The Early Years...

1998-2009

A TIP OF THE HAT COLLECTION

VOLUME 1

BOB 'IDEA MAN' HOOEY
Author of Legacy of Leadership

The early years... 1998-2009 A Tip of the Hat Collection of Idea-rich tips, thoughts, and ponderings from the creative mind of Bob 'Idea Man' Hooey

The early years... 1998-2009

A Tip of the Hat collection - 2 volume series – excerpts from 22-years of writing, thoughts and musings from **Canada's IdeaMan**, **Bob Hooey**

For 22 plus years I have wracked my brain to find something informative, provocative, or at least entertaining to share with my readers, clients, and subscribers. We even did an **Ideas At Work!** newsletter every month for 10 solid years.

In creating this book (two volumes) I decided to go though all those posts and articles and share a few that I felt might be of value to you. Enjoy!

Getting ready to host our 2013 Global Speakers Summit event.

The Global Speakers Summit foundation event was held in 2013 in Vancouver, BC. It was called, **The Music, The Magic, and The Message**. Our purpose was to continue supporting our CAPS Foundation as well as help start foundations in some of our other Global Speakers Federation member organizations. We were successful on both objectives. This was my final event as a member of our CAPS Foundation Board where I had served for the previous 5-years. I worked with my fellow board members to take us from an idea to a functioning foundation able to assist our speakers, should they need help.

When this project started, I didn't realize how much I had written over the years and ended up splitting the volume into two volumes. 1) The e**arly years** (1998-2009) and 2) **The saga continues** (2010-2019) and, who knows, perhaps there will be further volumes and maybe one final one called **The last years**. ☺

I trust you will be able to find something in this smorgasbord of ponderings. I've collected them by year and picked some of the better ones. Some ideas, some good news, some travel adventures… all in one place. A Tip of the Hat - enjoy!

Bob 'Idea Man' Hooey
Author, speaker, serial adventurer

1998-1999

1998: P*R*I*O*R*I*T*I*E*S

"A hundred years from now it will not matter, what size my bank account was, the sort of house I lived in, or the kind of car I drove...but the world may be different because, I was important in the life of a child."
Anonymous

Why is it that we wait until it too late to realize that our priorities are misplaced? We wait until our kids have grown up, without us. We wait until our spouse has had enough and is ready to leave us. We wait until our health is deteriorated, to the point of no return. No one on his or her deathbed ever said, **"Gee, I wish I'd spent more time at the office!"**

One **practical** suggestion to assist in regaining or getting effective control of your life would be being clear on your priorities in life, family, and business. Being focused on the priorities in your personal and family life makes it easier to blend them with your business, community, and career priorities and demands. Far too many people have paid too dear a personal price for having imbalanced priorities and have lost partners and families. This, all to common, personal tragedy can be avoided! It takes discipline, but it's worth it! **Wouldn't you agree?**

Someone told me, that to truly be effective in my life I should begin to **"schedule my priorities"** instead of just prioritizing my schedule, or to do lists. This **subtle** change in perspective has made a major difference in my life. This subtle change can make a difference in the results you experience along with life benefits.

Knowing what your priorities are and scheduling specific blocks of time to work on each of them each week, can free you up. **Steven Covey** built a whole course and publications around this universal concept. This helps you to say **"NO"** to demands that don't fall in line or distract you from seeing them fulfilled. You are better informed and able to evaluate decisions, time investment, and resource allotments towards specific goals. You can be more productive when you are working on the important projects in your career. You can be more fulfilled when you spend time with the important people in your life.

I'd suggest taking a few moments, on a regular basis, to go over your priorities. Plan to update, evaluate, or sometimes, even eliminate items entirely. You'll be glad you did! So will your friends and family.

Plan Monthly, Schedule Weekly and LIVE DAILY.

3

Take a moment and make a note to yourself about these various areas and your priorities in each. Then decide **which one is your highest priority**. Spend time later to refine and focus your thoughts. Keep your written priorities clear, concise, and focused. Then **schedule your priorities first!**

- **Family:**
- **Self-Improvement/Career Advancement:**
- **Work/Task:**
- **Spiritual/Personal:**
- **Community/Sports/Hobbies:**

1998: 48th Accredited Speaker in the history of Toastmasters

 I am privileged to be one of 48 speakers in the world to be able to wear this pin. It signifies that I have earned our most coveted, professional level, Accredited Speakers designation. (Update 2019 – there are now 87 Accredited Speakers) Visit **www.AccreditedSpeakers.com** for more information.

My journey started when I joined Toastmasters in April 1991. It moved forward in small steps (**small steps – BIG DREAMS**) when I got a flyer from Toastmasters International following achieving my Able Toastmasters. The flyer said, **ARE YOU GOOD ENOUGH TO BE A PRO?** I had it on the wall of my office and had written on it... **Not yet! But I will be!** It became a focus for my learning for the next year or two.

I believe you need to be a champion of your own **dreams** (turning them into reality). This is something experienced first-hand. I worked to overcome serious challenges and difficulties to prepare for the first level audition while working towards the Accredited Speaker designation. After passing level one I prepared for level two. There were times I thought about throwing in the towel. When I spoke in San Diego (1995) and was not successful, I pulled myself up and worked harder for my opportunity to speak the following year in Saint Louis.

When I again fell short, I was tempted to quit. I was frustrated, disappointed in my performance, and inclined to move on; to forget my dream of becoming a paid professional speaker. But something would not let me quit! My success team would not let me quit either. **They believed in me even when my belief wavered.** I took a year off as I was serving as District 21 Governor serving 195 Toastmasters clubs and our leaders. I would apply to speak the following year.

In 1998, when I *finally* walked across a Palm Desert, California stage to become the 48th person in the world to earn this coveted professional level Toastmasters International designation, I felt like a champion who had gone 10 rounds and emerged bloodied, but unbeaten. The applause and cheers of 2200 plus fellow Toastmasters still echo in my ears. It was a pinnacle point in my life as a professional speaker; the first of many.

If you would like to see it, follow this link: **https://youtu.be/5hyX_3wG468**

Was it the three speeches I prepared and presented on the TI world stage that earned this professional designation? Partially! Looking back, I believe it was the hundreds of prepared presentations given in various Toastmaster clubs and in community events across the country, as well as for paying clients that built the foundations for this eventual success on the world stage.

You can succeed in whatever field you enter if you are willing to prepare. You can become a top performing professional; be the champion you were meant to be. If I can do it, so can you!

1998: Travel the world… why not?

www.HaveMouthWillTravel.com

Back when I was just starting on my journey as a speaker I was asked about my goals. I was quick to share "I want to travel the world and share ideas that will help people live more effective lives and lead more dynamic teams and organizations." **Update 2019** Well, 25 years or so later, 71 countries on 6 continents doing presentations in 24 of them… I am seeing the results of all the preparation and practice over the years.

People today need help and they need hope. Essentially, **that is my business!**

I would love to come and work with you and your teams. Contact me at **bhooey@mcsnet.ca** or visit my website: **www.ideaman.net**

Mom and Dad at their 50th anniversary

1999: THANKS MOM!

I watched as my mom sat hunched in the second pew with my sister and brother-in-law. I was struck with how pale and small she looked. I was overwhelmed with love, overlaid with my own pain, as I saw her sitting there in quiet shock, tears streaming down her character lined face.

As I stood to speak in tribute to my father who had passed away earlier that week, I was overcome with the emotion of the day.

How would she cope without him, how would I cope without him? How would we fill the black hole left when he was taken from us?

I choked back my tears and began to speak; knees and voice trembling. I found my voice and was able to tell those in attendance just how much he had meant. To share stories of how he had taught me by quiet example; the values of honesty, of compassion, and of consideration for people regardless of their color or social standing. He would bring home millionaires and street people for a meal.

Of unconditionally loving his wife and kids; in sticking by us, despite some of the tough lessons I remember him facing. Of his steadfast faith and obedience to his God, and to his calling as an encourager. Of sharing the inscription, **"God's Friend"** I chose for him and felt was a worthy testimony to his life.

As speaker after speaker shared stories of my dad and the role he played in their lives, I was amazed at the impact he had on so many people. I wondered if he ever knew how much he had meant to so many. I wondered if anyone had ever told him.

I was humbled, yet comforted that the last words I had said to him the day before he died was **"luv you pop!"** Moreover, that the last message from him was how proud he and Mom were of me, and how much they loved me. Still makes me cry to think about him.

I was grateful that someone had challenged me earlier, to verbally acknowledge the important people in my life. Grateful that I had been able to share that love with Mom and Dad for the last 10-years we had together as adults.

Since that day, I constantly began consciously re-affirming my love and affection for my mom and sharing with her stories we have lived as a family. Stories which, upon reflection, form, in-part, the foundations for my life as it is today. Stories and lessons, which formed a foundation for some of the successes I have enjoyed of late. I am humbled and pleased that both my parents lived long enough to see some of their hard work and support pay off.

My mom was a wonderful woman! She had always been there for me; challenging me to be my best, in stretching past my comfort zone, in comforting me when I missed the mark either physically or psychologically. Along with my sister, I held her in my arms on August 20th, 1999 as she slipped away to join Dad in heaven. I am forever grateful for those last 6 months spent loving each other and sharing stories to inspire and encourage each other. My mom's legacy lives on in my writing as she constantly encouraged me to put pen to paper and capture and share my thoughts. A former English teacher, she was my first proof-reader. **Thanks Mom!** I remember her saying, **"Where did you learn to do this?"**

I decided to make sure that she understood just how much she had meant to me over the years. To make sure I was more diligent in my encouragement of my audiences to make time for the important people in their lives, and to acknowledge them NOW while they still have the chance.

As mothers' day approaches, I can simply say, **"THANKS MOM…. I still love you!" Update 2019**, all these years later I still miss you both!

1999: Take advantage of opportunities

Business at its essence is based on innovation, solving problems, and/or fulfilling the needs, wants, and desires of our clients.

Here's a potpourri sampler of how to take advantage of creative opportunities to build or **unlock your 'business' potential.**

- What business are you REALLY in? Keep asking this question and keep adapting your business to keep it fresh. Hint: think in terms of customer benefits. What do your customers get when they deal with you? What do they really want?

- Combine two or more products or services to create a new one. Perhaps you can work with a strategic partner or ally to develop a new service or product that will bring mutual benefit?
- Take an idea from another industry and transfer it or adapt to suit yours and the needs of your clients. (For example: air miles/coffee cards/buy 10 get one free promotions) Loyalty cards are everywhere now.
- Try something that didn't work the FIRST time. It might now; with changes in technology, resources, and client needs and attitudes.
- Take advantage of the trends or changing interest in the marketplace. This is where your customer service focus will help, a lot!
- Use a different material or process to do a traditional job. Creativity counts!
- Look for ways to be a value-added company or person, focusing on real customer service. How can you personally make changes to what you bring to your work?

Being creative is as simple as being open and being willing to risk by trying new or unfamiliar things and activities. Applied creativity is what solves your problems and builds your long-term business.

Looking at your business with fresh eyes, and from different perspectives is one secret in **unlocking your 'business' potential.**

1999: On Leadership

"Leadership," says **Peter Drucker** *"is lifting a person's vision to higher sights, raising a person's performance to a higher standard, and building a personality beyond its normal limitations."* Now that is creative vision!

The foundations of effective, personal leadership in a business, a career, or leading a volunteer group, start with 'each' person actively taking responsibility for their own actions as part of a group. Personal leadership precedes powerful, effective leadership in any role. Those foundations are enhanced in feeling confident enough to suggest, create ideas, and accept revisions in team goals and performance.

"Our productivity – often survival – does not depend solely on how much effort we expend, but on whether or not the effort we invest is in the right direction." We must create visionary, innovative road maps that will guide us and our colleagues to greater success. Lead on my friends!

1998-1999 A good starting point

Funny how things evolve as a writer. I remember being asked to do a course on **Listening Skills** for Langara College in Vancouver. They asked if I had a workbook to them to print. I said yes, glad that they were willing to do the printing. Then she said the magic words, "We will pay you $15 per workbook for each student!"

Pay me and do the printing!

I was blown away and a *light bulb* went off. If some one saw value in what I write to the point of paying for the privilege, perhaps I should stop devaluing what I created and start publishing and selling it too. I did!

I began by simply designing and printing a two-color cover for each of my workbooks and having them spiral bound for sale. And, they sold!

I had written I'm already running too fast! (1996), so updated it and it became my first one. Now renamed, **Running TOO Fast** is in its 8th edition as of this year.

My next two followed soon after in 1998; The secrets of EFFECTIVE Customer Service, now renamed, **Make ME Feel Special!** Now in its 6th edition (2019). As well, **Speaking for Success!** Now in its 9th edition (2020).

In 1999, I penned **Why Didn't I THINK of That?** Now going into its 6th edition in 2020. And many more… **see page 127** for more complete listing.

I created **Dad, You're still my hero!** shortly after he passed in 1999 and published **Thanks Mom!** on International Women's day shortly before she passed away.

In 2000, I discovered Create Space, now **Kindle Publishing**, and started conversion into full print books vs the workbook styles. We have been successful creating and publishing books in print, pdf, and e-pub formats ever since.

Visit www.SuccessPublications.ca to see the complete collection and order some for yourself, your friends, and your teams.

2000

2000: Ideas that are weird!

Innovation and idea generation are, in their very basics, about being curious and courageous... courageous about challenging the status quo and then making changes to make it better. This is where those who lead excel. They are not afraid to go outside the confines of their narrow field and to borrow, beg, and sometimes steal ideas from other fields and industries.

It is a good management practice to occasionally look at your norms and ask yourself the contrarian or flip side of the equation questions... this is where innovation and the real creative spark exist.

That doesn't mean you always throw away what you are currently using... at times it is still very effective and may be the most productive use of your time, resources, and energy. But what if there is a better way, a more productive way, a more cost-effective way... and your competitor finds it first? Hmmmmmm?

The secret to thriving in our competitive and, by now everyone understands, globally competitive market is in being **constantly on the 'improve'** and sometimes that means 'improv' to find the answers to the questions your existing and potential clients are asking. So, keep questioning and keep on the quest.

2000: What if...

What if you could have anything you wanted in life? **What if** you had all the talent, skills, money, and help you needed to accomplish your wildest dreams? **What if** you could find the solution to the challenge you face? **What if** you were really in charge of your life? What would you do? Where would you go? Who would you become?

Often, I encounter people mired in the day-to-day 'reality' who have forgotten how to dream. People who have had their dreams 'down-sized' by the dream killers among us; or eroded by the harsh demands of their environment and their on-going involvements.

Surprisingly, the answers we get in life are directly linked to the questions we ask! Ask the right questions and get different, more creative, more fulfilling answers. We accept the 'obvious answers' and settle for seconds when we could continue to ask for more and in turn receive more than we'd ever dreamed possible.

I will lead you through a few questions that I use personally in my search to see my dreams expanded and grounded in my future. This is the place to let your creative visualization skills run amok. Use soft background music to set the atmosphere for your mind to soar, to explore the creative possibilities these questions may spark.

This is a place where you need to be honest, without judgment; a place to let your imagination soar and explore the possibilities. Later we will cover how to integrate this section into your present-day reality and begin to see your dreams take form, as you build 'Foundations for Success' under them.

Relax! Let your mind flow and wrap your imagination around your future!

What if:

1. I was really in charge of my life, I'd:
2. I could do anything, without fear of failure, I'd:
3. I had enough money to ensure my basic living needs for a year, I'd:
4. I discovered I had the talent, could learn the skills I need to: _____, I'd:
5. Something I've always wanted to do is:
6. IF I could do anything, without limitations, I'd:
7. IF spoke as if (I thought) what was saying was important, I'd say:
8. I've always wanted to visit:
9. I've always wanted to learn how to:
10. I would like to leave a legacy of:
11. IF I could give my family anything, it would be:
12. IF I took full responsibilities for my choices, I'd:
13. IF I took full responsibility for my actions, I'd:
14. IF I were more accepting of: _____, I'd:
15. IF I took full responsibilities for my choice of companions, I'd:
16. IF I could have any career, without limitations, I'd
17. IF I had a dedicated support team to assist me, I'd:
18. IF God really cared and was willing to help me, I'd:
19. My greatest life goal is:
20. IF I could accomplish ONE thing before I pass on, I'd:

By now your mind should be whirling with endless possibilities. To explore those possibilities will be your choice of putting time and effort into **'doing your homework'**. To research and refine your dreams using these questions to unlock your power, to begin to dream again, and to act on those dreams will take courage and commitment. Believe me, it is so worth it!

2000: Leadership skills are changing... are yours?

If you truly seek to be an effective leader in 21st century, a reflective look at this list of leadership styles, activities, or attributes might be in order. **Ask yourself how many of these you exhibit** as you seek to lead those who have entrusted you with their concerns? What needs to change?

Responsible: Do you take full responsibility for your actions and decisions? Do you also take responsibility for their results?

Growing: Are you a leader on the grow, who is committed to seeking out new ideas, new methods, and new alliances to help serve those you lead? Are you a leader who is also a reader?

Exemplary: Do you walk your talk? Do your motives, actions, and attitudes reflect the character you would honestly like to become?

Inspiring: Do you inspire confidence and trust in those who follow you? Can you call them to action, to solve your mutual challenges?

Efficient: How are you on using your time wisely and the time of those you serve? Do they see you using your time in productive activities on their behalf? Do you have time to fully do your job?

Caring: Do your people know from experience that you care about them? Do you model it?

Communicating: How are you at sharing your ideas, at listening to the needs and concerns of your people, and in making sure that you fully understand them? Do you make sure they are well informed about what the challenges and your proposed solutions to those changes entail?

Goal oriented: Are you a leader who is effective in setting realistic goals, communicating those goals, gathering people to support the attainment of those goals, and who achieves the worthwhile goals set for the common good?

Decisive: Can you make an informed decision and act on that decision quickly? Do you study a challenge to death and continually put off deciding while waiting for more information?

Competent: This strikes at the heart of your ability to deliver the goods for your people. Are you competent to do the job and do it well?

Unifying: Are you a leader who seeks to include everyone involved and works hard to make sure no one is excluded? Are you a leader who builds bonds between diverse groups, many with conflicting agendas and viewpoints? Are you a leader who can earn their trust and allow them to get past their divisiveness and get behind you in accomplishing something which is for everyone's best interest? Are you a catalyst for commitment?

Working: Are you a leader who is committed to working on behalf of those who trust you? A leader who is not afraid to get their hands dirty, to dig in and lead by example, to do what is needed to get the job done successfully? Are you a leader who sets an energetic pace and is fully engaged on working out the solutions and to engaging people in the partnership of performance in achieving common goals?

Tough list isn't it?

If you truly seek to be a 21st century leader, these are the skills that will assist you in successfully serving and leading your people. **Are you willing to change?**

"The true mark of a leader is the willingness to stick with a bold course of action — an unconventional business strategy, a unique product – development roadmap, a controversial marketing campaign – even as the rest of the world wonders why you're not marching in step with the status quo. In other words, real leaders are happy to zig while others zag. They understand that in an era of hyper-competition and non-stop disruption, the only way to stand out from the crowd is to stand for something special." **Bill Taylor**

2001

2001: Secrets of a procrastinator - It's about time!

Next time, I'm not going to leave it until the last minute. Ever said that? I have and all too often – in the past! Ever notice how that happens? We start off with all sorts of good intentions and, somehow, we end up rushing, under pressure, stressed to complete a task that would have been a breeze, if ONLY, we had done it earlier.

"At times," said **Emerson**; *"the whole world seems to be in a conspiracy to importune you – with emphatic trifles."*

The **SECRET,** amid our often hectic, fast paced, activity driven life, is in our discerning and sidestepping those trivial demands. The secret is to remain focused and active.

"TODAY, is an important day!" according to fellow speaker **Zig Ziglar**, *"No matter how you spend it, you will have traded a day of your life for it!"*

Based on an improved age span of 85 years, we have **ONLY 31,046 days to LIVE!** Roughly 745,000 hours in which to live out our dreams, accomplish our life goals, and make an impact on our world and those with whom we share it. The secret in a productive life is in how we allocate this time.

"Do you love life? Then do not squander time." wrote **Benjamin Franklin**; *"For TIME is the stuff that life is made of."*

As a recovering PROCRASTINATOR, I offer these four suggestions to help control and conquer time and truly live your life.

- **DEVOTE** time to your goals. Make sure you know where it is you really want to go, what you really want to accomplish and what impact statement you want your life to make. Spend time analyzing, refining, and prioritizing. As little as 15 minutes a day could impact a lifetime. Make sure these goals are realistic and compatible with your life message. Then get on with them. **DO IT NOW!**

- **LEARN TO LEVERAGE** your time, by networking with others, by delegating or sharing tasks, by asking colleagues for help, and by seeking their energy, information, and resource sharing.

- **CREATE TIME** like **Thomas Edison**, who set aside a 'portion' of each day for creative processes. Use this time to Thunder-think, mind map goals and objectives, and to reflect on the organization, timing, and implementation of your goals. Use this creative time to dream and use visualization techniques to allow yourself to establish your own pace and direction.

- **DON'T WASTE YOUR TIME**. How many of us, could find at least 15-20 minutes a day that we now squander? According to **Goethe,** *"One always has enough time, provided one spends it well."* **What difference would that make?** Wasting or investing only 15 minutes a day works out to 91 hours per year. I'm told the typical college education requires about 2400 hours to complete. These small **seemingly 'insignificant'** minutes, if reclaimed and invested wisely over the course of your life, could give you the equivalent of and 'advanced' education, in a field of your choosing. Would this make a difference in your career path? **I would say YES!**

Secrets of a recovering procrastinator

For example, if we read an average of twelve pages a day (about 15 minutes), we could easily read 17-18 career focused books per year. Considering the North American average is ONLY ONE NON-FICTION BOOK PER YEAR – you might begin to see the competitive advantages.

- In one year, anyone of us could become a local authority in our field of study, in less than three years an expert, and potentially – in just under five years, an **internationally acclaimed authority in that field of study.**

- We can enjoy a definite advantage or an edge for success if we are well read. Reading BROADENS our experience and expands our possibilities. Statistics show that approximately 40% of North American adults are not 'fully' capable of reading even their daily working material. Only 15 minutes a day could effectively teach them the fundamentals of reading and make a major impact in their lives and their employment prospects.

- Or, these same **'insignificant'** minutes could help us get into and stay in shape while tuning up our heart. I'm told just 15 minutes of cardio-vascular (aerobic style) activity – 3 times a week is all we really need to maintain a healthy body. INTERESTING! Only 15-minutes, you say? Hmmm…maybe tomorrow?

- Perhaps these **'insignificant'** minutes would well be spent or invested in personal mediation or spiritual contemplation, helping to bring your soul, mind, and spirit into balance.

- Maybe, these **'mini-moments'** could be shared exclusively with your family or close friends engaging in real, quality communication to create and build healthy life-long relationships?

"Don't waste time," writes Australian Pioneer **Arthur Brisbane**, ***"Don't waste it regretting the time already wasted... you have time enough left (for some accomplishment and recovery) if you will but use it... while life and time remain."***

Your life and time management remain in your hands. It is within your power to choose to invest it well for your benefit and the benefit of those you love. Or, you can choose to let others rob you of your life's blood or squander it on useless pursuits. **It is your choice – and it's about time!**

2001: The Greatest Gift!

December is a month of hectic activity. For North American retailers, it is traditionally a month that can make the difference in their fiscal year.

For the rest of us in business it can be very busy as well. It will be for me... as I write this, I am in Halifax for the 1st of three presentations.

Not everyone celebrates Christmas, but most of us at least *pause* to reflect on 'gifts' during this tremendously *commercial* part of the year. I'd like to challenge each of you to consider the greatest gift of all.

Picture: Bob and Santa Barry

Danny Thomas said, **"*Success in life has nothing to do with what you gain in life or accomplish for yourself. It's about what you do for others.*"**

Wise words from a very successful entertainer, investor, and community supporter. Wise words for those of us in business as well. Isn't 'giving' the essence of what makes the successful business grow?

16

What is the greatest gift you may be thinking? Well, I believe the greatest gift we can give is our appreciation and recognition that we care.

- Have you told your family that you appreciate their contributions and support over the past year? *Their gifts of love and support.*
- Have you told your friends and colleagues the same thing?
- How about your staff who have worked with you this year to build or work through the challenges together? *Their gifts of diligence, support, and value-added contributions.*
- How about your suppliers who helped you and were consistent in making sure you had what you needed to serve your clients? *Their gifts of service and support for your efforts.*
- How about the most important people in your *business* life – your customers? *Have you let them know how much you appreciate the gift of their trust in doing business with you lately?*

My challenge for each of you is to *take a moment* and reflect on the people who have given you the gift of their friendship, love, and support and then find some way to let them know.

2001: Creativity Corner

I moved out here in 2000 and have this as part of my address on my driver's license. When I moved here there were no house numbers or street signs, so I made mine up. The post office is ok with it, **10, Creativity Corner, Egremont, AB T0A 0Z0**. My mail gets here on a regular basis (we have a box, mine is Box 10) and it often is a conversation starter with people as I travel. Truth be told, my clients don't really care where I am coming from – they just want to know I can get to where they are! And, I do!

17

2002

2002: 10 steps to a better '_____' business

The following ideas have proven effective for the Business enhancement success of 'any' business. Fill in the _____ with your field, and apply accordingly. However, since I am *primarily* in the speaking and training business, I will share ideas drawn from what I am learning in my quest to make what I do more productive and profitable. Ideas to make sure I stay competitive in this growing global field. I am sure you will be able to see how you can apply them to your specific areas of concern.

Use client testimonials:

People hire speakers and trainers based on several factors: They have heard us speak personally; someone they trust has heard us; or another speaker, trainer, or client has heard us and says nice things about what we did for them. **They do not normally hire on the basis of a cold call**. They may, if the timing is correct, but will still go back to one of the above three factors as a part of their decision process.

This applies to any business format, and is important, as it helps **minimize the risk factor** in the decision process to engage or do business with us. How can you ensure your clients talk about what you've done for them? How do you get them to do so? Who have you successfully served who would be willing to tell the world what a great job you did? Ask them! Thank them!

Two points: 1) Do a simply outstanding job and **keep in touch** afterwards – remember out of sight out of mind equals out of business and; 2) Ask them to give you feedback on what you did and how it affected or assited them in their business. Ask for quantified answers, if you can get them, as they are more effective tools. Ask permission to quote them! Many will say yes!

Make your website a value added resource:

If you are not already on-line, you are positoned to be be left behind in your potential client's mind. The internet is beginning to replace the yellow pages as a form of research for client use. **2019 update** – it has!. It is becoming a source of credibity as well as visibility. Start with making sure you are on-line and that your website covers the basics: Who you are? What you do? What you offer? What people say about you? Then move into the process of making your website a resource base that people will want to put on their favorites and return again and again. Have some articles or tips that will help them. Include some inspiration. Give more information on the behind the scenes workings of your business or services. If you visit my **IDEAS AT WORK!** site (www.ideaman.net) you'll see some of these examples; with my 'Collection of Wisdom' downloadable articles from North America's top experts, and **B**usiness **E**nhancement **S**uccess **T**ools.

I've found this to be one of the most productive things I've done to assist my potential clients sine 1998 when we lauched the ideaman.net site. The majority of my promotion directs people to my site, as it is a great sales tool. It works very well!

Build rapport with clients... teach or provide something new:

I got my start in the speaking and training business quite a while back, when I was a kitchen designer, by offering in-house and continuing education programs to assist my potential clients in their quest for a better kitchen. Along the way I wrote, **"How to Remodel Your Kitchen & Stay Married!"** *as a tool to help them prepare and survive the marriage stretching kitchen rennovation.*

In business, we are more successful when percieved as value-added or solutions-oriented. Make sure they see that you are there to help them and are committed to their success. I thank my clients for allowing me to be a part of their success team in their training program or conference. It is a statement of commitment on my part and a reminder to me to always seek to add value and build on the relationship. Hey, and it certainly helps with the referrals as well.

Promote your delivery timelines and other uniquenesses:

Do you have something special you do in relation to how quickly you can respond, or deliver a service or deliver on a request? Is there a way to capitalize on something you do and do consistently well? Considere the Domino's Pizza lesson in revamping the Pizza delivery concept.

Here's a tip for speakers and trainers: Are you available to fill-in for a speaker who cannot make it, can you market to your local convention market on this basis? Might not be a bad idea to become known to the local convention market and hotels with convention space. **They get asked for referrals!** If they know you, they might just promote you!

One of the ways I am servicing this market is in the use of my **"How to Host a Successful Meeting, Training Session, or Convention"** which uses some of the custom checklists and resource materials developed to help the meeting planner. This fall I intend to use it as a contact for the local hospitality market in the Edmonton region, where I now have a creative hide-away in the country. **Update 2019**: we edited and expanded it for 2020 as **Maximize Meetings**. Visit **www.successpublications.ca** to order your personal copy.

Co-promote with strategic alliances:

Our global enconomy is getting more competitive on an hourly basis. **If they don't know you, how will they find you?** And how will they know to hire you? This is a challenge that faces every type of business professional, in that they must find an effective way to get through the overload of 'messages' bombarding their potential clients, tell their stories, and entice or inspire them to make contact. Working together is a tool that is underutilized.

One of the interesting things is seeing former competitors joining forces to co-promote where previously they would not have even said good morning. This can be a very effective tool as you get to know other professionals in your field and what they offer. As a speaker, I have found that 'speakers promote speakers' and have had specific referrals that have turned into speaking engagements. I've also had the privilege of being able to do the same for fellow speakers within CAPS and NSA, and do gladly when I know they will do a good job for the client. Again, it is a matter of referral based on professionalism in the field.

On a simply accounting point of view, it makes promotional work feasible as well. Speakers work together to produce co-op newsletters, Web-sites, advertisements in meeting planner guides, brochures, boot camps, and anthologies which can be a nice augment to your product offering as well. **www.AlbertaSpeakers.com**

Use business discussion and news groups:

These internet-based groups are a source of business research and if you are careful a source of subtle self-promotion and awareness. For example, LinkedIn and Facebook have focused groups. A word of caution here, don't be overtly commercial as it will backfire on you big time!

Sell an inexpensive introductory product:

If you are in a position that you have a product line, make it easy for people to start dealing with you. Find something that they will enjoy using and get them on your client list. **Perhaps you can also offer something for free to get them hooked?** Not necessarily a 'loss leader' but something that is inexpensive and will demonstrate your ability to deliver when you say you will, and to introduce them to what you have to offer. **Update 2019**: I use my 'kindle shorts' books for this purpose. People seem to appreciate them!

Personalize with your picture:

People like to deal with real people. Even if your business is internet based, they like to know that there is a **real person** behind the product or service they acquire from you. As speakers and trainers especially, we are in the personal services business.

Make sure it is a current picture and that it shows you smiling. It helps if they don't ask you where your son is when you show up at the airport or the venue! ☺

Personalize your business – you'll be glad you did!

Up-sell to all of your clients... add-on, premium, extras, and related items:

This is one of three success secrets of generating additional business and increasing your bottom line. Design what you offer so you can provide a choice of at least three levels: **good, better, best – and then offer it to each client**.. Give them a choice with at least 3 alternatives. Make sure each is value added and meets their needs.

Don't be afraid to ask for the order and the upgrade… remember a simple, **"would you like fries with that?"** has made MacDonald's very profitable. Look for ways to add other items to your product or service mix that will be a benefit to your clients. Can you offer consulting, facilitation, team training, executive debriefing sessions, panel moderation, company spokesmanship, or multiple sessions that save your clients additional airfare and expenses? **If so, then offer them!** Remember your goal is to help them improve their life or business. What do you offer that will do that?

Bonus: Ask for referrals:

Here is the business building secret of the sales superstars, and in every field of business. **"Who else do you know that would benefit or be interested in what I offer?"** Why is we often work dilligently to get their business and then, after we have knocked their socks off with our superb execution, that we fall short of asking them to share us with those they know and care about?

Ask, and ye shall receive!

2002: "And now our Canadian Ambassador from Vancouver, British California…" (and yes, they said British California ☺)

"Gulp, why did I agree to do this," I thought, as I was being introduced at a meeting of the National Speakers Association in Los Angeles, California. (1999) After all, who was I to be speaking to this august gathering of some of North America's top speakers and trainers?

The thunderous applause spurred me on, helping me get past my initial stage fright and I walked on to see 640 cheering speakers (and a few Canadians interspersed throughout the crowd.) Conference chair, **Janet Lapp, CSP** had asked us as Canadian Speakers to host the Saturday night event for this annual gathering and I had somehow been appointed official Canadian Ambassador to the NSA for this event.

We had done ourselves proud with Canadian flag pins, Canadian Airlines in-flight magazines and snacks at every place, and Canadian Flags (large and small) throughout the room. I stopped and took a deep breath before speaking. "Remember, they are just like you," I told myself. "But I have some of their books and tapes!" I pressed on.

I simply shared that we **Canadian Association of Professional Speakers** members were glad to be here and to help celebrate our continued friendship and the co-founding of the Global Speakers Federation (1997). I told them of the border crossing at Blaine, where it says, **"Children of a common mother"** and I asked those Canadians in the audience to stand and be recognized. Fourteen people from across Canada stood to a thunderous applause that lasted for minutes.

I had my eyes opened that day, as did my fourteen fellow Canadians. We often miss the respect and esteem in which we are held outside our country.

People look at us and are impressed by the quality we bring to our work and the commitment to our craft across the world. It was nice for that moment to share that honor and that sense of appreciation with my fellow Canadians.

2002: Canada, the world's funniest country… eh?

People think Canadians are a serious people and we are, about our beer, our hockey, and our politics. Ok, maybe I lied about the politics, eh?

I was sitting in the Edmonton's Citadel Theatre one night watching a 75-year old man bounce around the stage keeping the audience totally entertained as he talked and joked about Canada and all things Canadian.

I refer, of course, to that great Canadian icon and fellow CAPS member **Dave Broadfoot**, CSP. For more than two hours he entertained us with stories and word plays that poked fun at our politicians, our food, our ethnic diversity, our sports, and our sense of humour. And I wasn't the only one with sore sides when I left.

It got me thinking about our great country. **Why is Canada great, you may ask?**

My feeling is our sense of humour is rooted in not taking ourselves too seriously. One of the things I've noticed as I work with business leaders across Canada, is the more successful they are, the less seriously they take themselves and the more likely they are to tell jokes about themselves, too. Perhaps Canada is a bit more mature about life than many of our fellow countries. Perhaps we are just a little more *fun to be around* in the first place.

- Where else would we have a TV show called "This hour has 22 minutes" whose only premise is to take pokes and jokes at our expense?
- Where else would this show be funded by public money and aired on our own Canadian Broadcasting Corporation to millions of Canadian taxpayers every week?

Canada is a great place to live because of the people who live here. **People, who are willing to look at themselves, see the humour and share that humour with the world.** And, I'm not kidding!

"I am deeply moved by the warmth and courage of the Canadian people which I felt so strongly during my recent visit to your country. Your support of the struggle against apartheid restored me in my journey home and reassured me that many just people around the world are with us."
Desmond Tutu

2002: My favorite Canadian...

With Fathers' Day just passed, I got thinking about my dad and how important he was in my life and development. I still miss him terribly! If I could, I'd nominate him as the Greatest Canadian in our history, at least in mine. Let me tell you why.

Ronald Howard Hooey February 11th, 1917 to February 11th, 1999

My dad was born on a farm in outside of Regina, Saskatchewan (Estevan area), the only son with 7 older sisters. His father died young, so he worked and helped around the farm and in town after they sold the farm. He worked and went to school until the 2nd world war where he volunteered for the air force even though he could have sat it out due to his family responsibilities. **He was committed to freedom and to this concept we call Canada and was willing to risk his life in its defense.**

Toward the end of the war he visited Olds, Alberta with my mom's brother, **Ralph Shackleton**, and the match was struck; a love affair that lasted 55 years until death finally separated them. After the war they adopted my sister and me, as they were not able to have any kids of their own. They chose to make a home for us and to nurture us as we grew into adulthood.

My dad never received any fame or fortune when he was alive, received few awards for service (and he served faithfully and fully), never made a lot of money, or left a huge fortune to my mom or us kids. He was never elected to office or did anything overtly newsworthy. **Why would I say he was the greatest Canadian I ever knew?**

Ronald Howard Hooey had a heart and a soul as vast and giving as our county has diversity in its landscape and ethnic blending!

Dad positively loved people and was no respecter of position, treating everyone he met with respect and hospitality. He was, and is in my memory, the quintessential Canadian role model. Giving, loving, hard-working, genuine, family oriented, forgiving, industrious, and above all loyal and dedicated to making this country better because of his life.

I have a fantastic *standard* to inspire me and to challenge me as I travel North America and the globe sharing my ideas with my audiences. A standard, I would wish everyone would seek to emulate and build on. **If we could each follow his example, this country would truly be the greatest country in the world and then some.** Sadly, he left us on February 11, 1999, but his memory and his inspiration remain.

2002: Hey, you must know...?

Have you ever had one of our neighbours to the south or someone from another country ask you if you knew their friend, cousin, uncle, or some other relative when they found out you were from Canada? Interesting how little they know about the vastness of Canada or where our cities and towns are in relation to each other.

I live part of the time in the Greater Vancouver area and have a quiet place in the country north of Edmonton where I go to relax and do some of my creative writing between trips. As a professional speaker, I am frequently on the road to some Canadian city and occasionally south of the border sharing my **Ideas At Work!** with our American cousins. **Update 2019** – I now live full time in the country here in Alberta and travel the globe from here. (61 countries, so far.)

It never ceases to amaze me, when they ask me if I know someone in Toronto, Montreal, or Halifax. I also find their reactions vary when I tell them how far these places are from where I live, and that 100,000 or 1,000,000 people live in the area they ask about.

I guess we should forgive our American cousins.☺ After all, as Canadians we all too often forget how vast and varied our country is in climate, population, people and ethnic mix. I encourage my Canadian friends to travel this great country and visit their 'extended family' to see for themselves just how great a place we call home.

I've had the pleasure of travelling coast-to-coast and visiting most of the Provinces, and last year two visits to the Yukon or my more recent trip to the North West Territories. This is an awesome place.

So, the next time someone asks, **"Hey, you must know?"** take a moment to reflect and share the greatness that is our home. Perhaps take the time to share the greatness of our country with the person who says it.

2003

2003: Dark contrasts

You could see the marks left by her tears in her dirty and haggard face. The fear and distrust were easily read in the way she sat and looked at you. Such a lot of sorrow in a 12-year-old girl's face. But, if I had seen my mother and older sister dragged off to be beaten, raped, and killed I think I would be the same. Or, if I had run for my life, hiding out and only travelling at night eating what I could find or dig up along the way, I might better understand.

"Mom, I don't have anything to wear," she cried. Her mom came up and opened the closet to pull out several new outfits. "But mom, I want to wear my green jumpsuit." Later at breakfast she complained about the choice of jams for her toast.

Two 12-year-old girls, one living in war torn Bosnia, and one living safely in Richmond, BC.

What a dark contrast in their lives and the challenges they face as they mature into womanhood. Will the little girl from Bosnia even get a chance to mature?

As Canadians, we too often take for granted the richness we share and the abundance that surrounds us. Go visit a grocery store and take a moment to decide what kind of milk or cheese or meat you'd like to buy for dinner and remember that somewhere in the world there are people who have no such choice.

Take a walk in your local park and enjoy the warmth of Canada Day, or any day, with your family. But remember somewhere there are people who cannot walk freely for fear of being shelled, beaten, raped, or shot.

This Canada Day take a moment and remember the greatness we share and say a prayer of gratitude that we live in this wonderful country of ours. There are so many valid reasons why the UN still says Canada is the most desirable country to live in, and why 1000's of people, every year, risk their lives in an attempt to reach our shores. Enjoy the contrast but work to keep it a safe place for us to share and to open our arms and our hearts to help those who don't have the good fortune to live here.

2003: Observing the speed limits

Most of us, if given enough time to think about it, would realize what truly enriches our lives, what makes us happy, gives us joy and a sense of purpose or pastes a grin on our chin. Our problem – we are driving too fast to even notice! We're so busy working overtime, meeting deadlines, chasing career opportunities, and running yellow lights that **we don't notice.** The things we value, that bring true riches to our lives, are lost in the blur. The hectic pace at which we live is costing us more than we realize; often what we say we value the most!

As we crowd each day with more work and activities than it can suitably hold, a heavy penalty is extracted for resisting our impulses to rest. If I can only get this project done, if I can only land this contract, if I can only... then I can rest. As a speaker and trainer, I am constantly stretched in this area. Left in our wake, amongst the swirling dust are our friendships, our health, our family, and our connection with our maker.

When I was somewhat younger, I remember saying (after watching my folks and their age group) that **"I'd rather burn out than rust out!"** Boy was I wrong, and arrogant too! That attitude and the speed in which I, like many of my generation, pursued my dreams and careers, led me to a premature burn out, and the loss of a marriage and a business I loved. A harsh lesson to be learned for **not observing the speed limits in my life**. I have applied and built on the lessons from this experience, and share them as I travel the globe, challenging my audiences to seek increased productivity and add some real balance in their lives and careers.

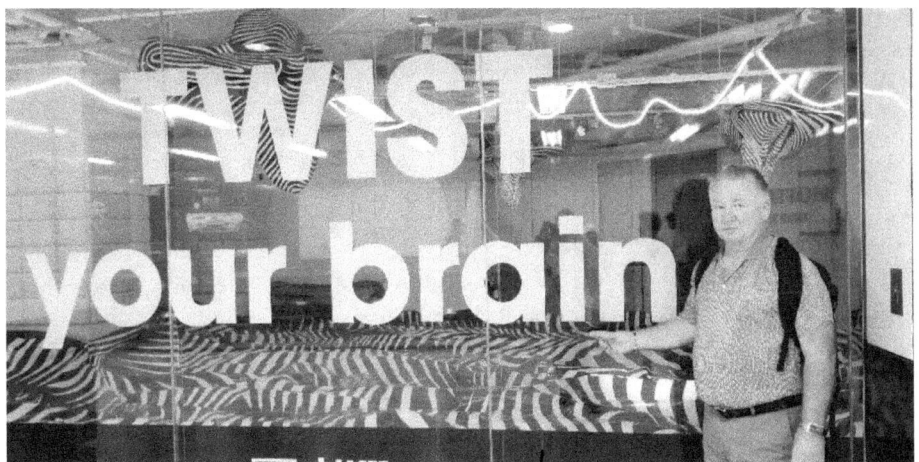

We are living too fast, and the casualties are piling up along our causeways. In 1976 there were 3.3 million single-income, two-parent families here in Canada.

In 1998, even with our population growth, there were only 1.8 million. We are losing ground! Only 58% of Canadians take any holidays from June to September – way down from 76% in 1992. Our excessive speeding is having an impact on our families, and those we love most, our kids. **It's killing our communities.** People hardly have time to stop and talk with their neighbors anymore. Been broken into lately? Wonder why no one saw anything? **No one was home!** We were all so busy speeding off to a meeting or to work.

Slowing down in a speeded-up world is not quitting your career or abandoning your dreams and your desire to provide for your family. **Making an impact** in this world requires that we slow down at least long enough to focus on the things, which matter most, and the people we love.

There are times when we simply must grab the wheel, gulp our latte's and drive. But more importantly, there are times when it is deadly serious to pull over in a rest stop, and rest for a while. Time to pull over and take a walk, to think and reflect on our life and our destination. Time to make sure we are heading in the right direction. We may be making good time and progress; but are we working towards a goal that matters to us, that makes sense for our families, and that adds value to our communities?

Pull over and give these questions some thought! You will be glad you did!

2003: I was allergic to hay…

Bob and sister Patti-Robin

Growing up I wanted to be a cowboy like **Roy Rogers**. Turns out I was allergic to hay… so I became a professional speaker instead. ☺

I remember watching shows like Gun Smoke, the Lone Ranger, Rifleman, and my favorite, **Have Gun Will Travel** starring **Richard Boone**.

It was good to have role models and heroes as a kid. Whether it was at the movies on a Saturday afternoon or sitting, mesmerized, in front of a small black and white TV, I was hooked. I wanted to be 'that' cowboy riding in to face down the bad guys, to be the one who brought hope and help to the town folk or business owners. **Well, I am that now!**

28

2004

2004: COWBOYS AND COMMUNICATION

A cowboy gets up everyday and knows he has a job to do… to get a herd of reluctant, independently thinking cows across the prairie to a siding, where they will be shipped to market. He gains satisfaction from doing his job well, and will continue to do so today, and tomorrow, and the day after that… because he is a cowboy! Along the way, he will battle unforgiving elements, sickness, boredom, balking cows, demanding terrain, and loneliness.

In our search as professional speakers, to become effective communicators, we too will encounter numerous challenges… challenges that, when overcome, will become the very foundations for our continuing success!

A cowboy doesn't think anything special about his skills and talents in roping, cutting, riding, or throwing; he just uses them as part of his daily tools in doing his job. Similarly, with our communication skills, we need to take them into our daily lives and workplace to become truly proficient and effective in their use.

Our audiences deserve our best! This is the essence of true professionalism! This is the secret of Toastmasters, CAPS, and NSA in helping us to reach our goals and our audiences.

A cowboy doesn't whine when he comes to a detour or problem. He doesn't cry when his horse throws him. He gingerly picks himself up, dusts himself off, and gets back on again. When he comes to a dry hole, he simple mounts his horse and rides on in search of a well to water himself and his livestock.

Neither should we whine when we go through a dry spell; a relationship that doesn't work, a business that doesn't perform, or a speech that doesn't quite come off as well as we'd planned. We can, like the cowboy, simply pick ourselves up, refocus our energies, and move on in search of our future success!

A cowboy is the quintessential role model of the entrepreneurial communicator; in choosing his words carefully, planning and executing his actions wisely, and persistently focusing his energies on the job at hand. He listens slowly to hear the hidden meaning and then acts with confidence. We can learn well from this role model and can apply these same traits and dedications to our own success as speakers and communicators. Our audiences deserve our best!

This was originally penned in 1995 when I spoke at a special Western Themed event in Kamloops, BC

2004: Mistakes... leverage for success!

"Crisis can often have value because it generates transformation...
I have found that I always learn more from my mistakes than from my
successes. If you aren't making some mistakes, you aren't taking enough
chances." **John Sculley**

Like many of you, I hate making mistakes, and, worse yet, having to admit them and clean up after them. This has often been an area of challenge for me in my growth as a person and in establishing my business. I am still learning and that is the important thing.

Someone told me, *"Learn from the mistakes of others, you'll never live long enough to make enough of your own."* At the time, that sounded ludicrous, as I didn't want to admit my own, let alone discuss them with someone else, or hear about theirs.

A while back while flying to a speaking engagement in the USA I read an article about a company who had tackled this *'mistake-itis'* full-on and had turned it into a value-added training tool for their company. What they did was invite their management and staff to submit their mistakes and each month they voted on the biggest mistake and gave a decent cash prize for the *'winner.'*

Initially I thought, *"What a dumb idea!"* But, as I finished reading the article, I saw the wisdom in their process. What they had discovered was needless repetition of mistakes throughout the company, were costing them needless manpower and additional resources. Someone would make a mistake, fix it, and simply continue without talking about it. In fact, the corporate climate was such that mistakes were not openly discussed. Then someone else would repeat the mistake, etc.

"A mistake only proves that someone stopped talking long enough to do something." **Michael LeBoeuf**

The positive results of developing a culture where mistakes were accepted as a *'normal'* part of doing the work and in making progress were amazing. The **sharing of the mistakes, and the lessons learned was the key point.** Sharing mistakes and the lessons, *'leveraged'* the learning curve of their management and their staff. It allowed them to avoid needless repetition of mistakes, and all the lost time and costly resources that entailed. It allowed the company to grow and expand on a stronger foundation. It encouraged its management and staff to be more open to innovation and to take *'educated'* risks in developing new business, services, and products to serve their changing clientele.

- What was your most recent mistake?
- What did you learn from it?
- Have you shared the lesson you learned with your team?

One of my biggest, value-added, lessons in life was in learning how to not *'recycle'* my mistakes. To learn from each one, savour the lesson, and move ahead boldly to make some new mistakes. And some new progress!

2004: Hey didn't you used to be Bob Hooey?

My response, **"Yes, but I'm better now!"** ☺ I turned to see this face smiling at me across the Tim Hortons in Edmonton where I had stopped for a coffee to await Irene's return from Banff.

Wayne Land, (*pictured here*) reintroduced himself to me and reminded me that we had gone to Queen Elizabeth High School together in the mid-60's. I was surprised he recognized or remembered me from that many years back. We traded cards and promised to get together.

Well, my 'old' friend Wayne (after all, he is a month older than me ☺) and I have been meeting for coffee or breakfast on average once a month since then. We've traded stories of our years in High School, our adventures since then. Our lives, our medical challenges as we get older, and, of course, to encourage each other as well. He reminded me that he knew my parents as they would often stop and pick up his sister on the way to drop Mom off at Edmonton's Victoria Composite High School.

He has become one of my biggest cheerleaders and seems to enjoy reading (FB posts) and hearing about my travels and my writing. **Update 2019**: I will make sure he gets a copy of this latest project when it is published in 2020. We continue our breakfast meetings and our friendship.

It is nice to have someone from your past become a part of your present and hopefully a part of our shared future. Wayne says "According to the internet I will live to be 90. We will be friends for another 30 years… and that must be true, as the internet doesn't lie… does it?"

2005

2005: My friend Bev Baker-Hoffman shared a few ideas for gifts for that special person. One size fits all.

The gift of wisdom,
the gift of encouragement,
the gift of inspiration,
the gift of hope,
the gift of time,
the gift of a listening ear,
the gift of compassion,
the gift of kindness,
the gift of appreciation,
the gift of optimism,
the gift of humour,
the gift of loyalty,
the gift of strength,
the gift of courage,
the gift of connection,
the gift of faith,
the gift of respect,
the gift of honesty,
the gift of forgiveness,
and the gift of patience.

I would add one more to this list, the gift of friendship.

I have been blessed with many fine supportive friends... and wanted to remind you that the gift of friendship is one that keeps giving all year long.

2005: *"I hear and I forget.*
I see and I remember.
I do and I understand!"
Confucius

These *wise words* were written thousands of years ago and yet they ring just as true in our 21st century lives and evolving business endeavors.

We *best equip* those we lead with use-it-now information, practical tools, and applicable actions, *when we facilitate* them to get their hands *dirty* or get up and use what we provide.

For example: In our on-site presentation skills training or executive speech coaching programs, the quicker we get the students or clients up speaking, the better they learn and accelerate their learning curve. Consider the thousands of Toastmasters around the world who *nervously* start speaking and find that their confidence and competence increases in *direct* relation to how often they are in front of an audience and in how they *apply* the feedback received. Becoming an effective presenter is not learned *exclusively* from a book or observing others in action. It is essentially a learn as you do project. Kind of like life!

My challenge for you is to revisit what you are doing for your own learning curve, as well as those you work with… see where you can adapt it to add more *hands-on* experience. How can you make it more experiential to anchor the learning and enhance the skill? Visit **www.ideaman.net** for information on our programs.

2005: How would you choose to be remembered?

The earlier part of this year (2005) saw the loss of some close Toastmaster friends, as well as my next-door neighbor, **Ron Bigoray**, who was only 2 years older than me. I spoke at Ron's service and reminded the family and friends of his many gifts, our great times of shared laughter and love.

Last week, I attended a funeral of a 96-year old member of my *extended family*… my brother-in-law's aunt and grandmother to a close friend.

Makes you think! When you lose someone close to you, it challenges you, in a very deep way, to re-examine your own life and activities. I know in 1999, when both my parents passed away, I made some serious and substantial changes in my life, my business and how I invest my time.

"This is the true joy in life: Being used for a purpose recognized by yourself as a mighty one, being a force of nature instead of a feverish, selfish little clod of ailments and grievances, complaining that the world will not devote itself to making you happy. I am of the opinion that my life belongs to the whole community and as long as I live, it is my privilege to do for it what I can. **It is a sort of splendid torch which I have got hold of for the moment, and I want to make it burn as brightly as possible before handling it on to future generations.***"* **George Bernard Shaw**

I keep this quote on the wall, so it gets seen on a frequent basis. It serves as a visual reminder of my own desire to make sure I, too, burn brightly and give solid value in everything I do.

Fellow author, speaker and *former* Edmontonian, **Brian Tracy** shared his wish to be remembered. His choice, *"Brian Tracy had a profound and positive influence on improving the lives of millions of people."* From what I gotten to know of Brian over the years, it appears he is making this a reality.

My challenge for you is to revisit how you would choose to be remembered. I wish each of you a long and productive life. Productive is a subjective term – so however you define it – you can create it!

However, each of us has a specific time here on earth to accomplish what we may. We can choose to make a statement with our life and the legacy or legend that we create in living it. **What is your choice?**

2005: What do you wish for?

Ever notice how you often get what you wish for? Life is funny at times!

More so, when you are *in business for yourself* and have *some* leadership control over where you choose to invest your time. There are times when you are so busy you really don't know where one project ends, and another starts, and you wish for some breathing room. Have you ever caught yourself feeling this? Amazingly enough, you often get that wish. Why? It is due to your being *too busy* working *in* the business, to work *on* the business.

- By working *on the business*, I mean spending time in strategic planning and development of new services, products, and profit areas.
- By working *on the business*, I mean investing time marketing and promoting what you do to current and prospective clients.
- By working *on the business*, I mean investing time and resources in your own growth and skills development.
- By working *on the business*, I mean investing time in strategic play and creative indulgence. This will energize both your mind and your body.

When you are working *in* **the business**, your focus is on doing the jobs, engagements, projects that you have committed to doing... at times, just keeping up or keeping your head above water. The result of not investing time to work *on* **the business** is the gigantic roller coaster of cash flow and client engagement.

If you study **North America's top companies and their leaders** you'll find out they take regular time to *strategically* work on their businesses, to work on developing their teams and enhancing their skills, and to tweak what they are doing and to make it better. They also take regular time to relax, unwind, and recharge their mental and physical batteries.

2005: Are you taking advantage of all your opportunities to be happy?

"I don't know what your destiny will be, but one thing I do know, the only ones among you who will be really happy are those who have sought and found how to serve." **Albert Schweitzer**

Are you happy in your career or business? Does it show?

Many of us miss amazing opportunities to bring a little joy into the lives of our customers, and through that ourselves, when we forget why we are in business. I tell my audiences that, **"*the main purpose of business is to make the lives of our customers better, at a profit.*"**

I had the privilege of sharing these and other thoughts for **Edmonton's Business Link.** We broke new ground as we video cast this presentation to 17 other centers across Alberta and Saskatchewan. I got to lead this initiative.

When we are too focused on the daily challenges of dealing with conflicting demands, customer quirks, and the hectic pace in which we live and do business, it is easy to forget. We lose the joy and zeal we had when we first started. This is a downward spiral making life more difficult and our relationships less satisfying. This spiral can be *easily* halted and reversed. It's a matter of perspective and choice!

Our success in business and life is built on relationships. Those relationships are enhanced and enriched when we reach out and touch people. I had the opportunity to visit with my friend **Eric Chester**, CSP when he was presenting here in Edmonton. Eric is the authority on dealing with **Generation Why?** He has a new book out *"Getting them to give a damm"* that we'll be reviewing in the future.

"There is a great paradox in reaching out to touch someone – and that is, the more you reach out to others, the more you will be touched yourself. Joy and happiness in great measure are waiting for us if we will reach just a little further," writes **Joan Rawlusyk.**

My challenge for you is to make a conscious effort to reach out and touch the people who come into your life personally and in your business. Be open to sharing joy and happiness in what you do.

If you're curious about me and these two kids… a few years ago I had the great opportunity to work with two delightful grade 3 students – **Astounding Announcers**, who were introducing the speakers (including me) at a CAPS Edmonton event I was hosting.

They were so much fun and a joy to work with… and they were very good too! Got me inspired to push myself in polishing my craft. I bet they will go on to create greatness in life.

2005: So now what?

Fall is now upon us and the summer is a softly fading memory. The days are growing shorter, the leaves are turning colour, and some are shedding already. Now what? Where do you go from here?

Henry R. Luce who published "Time," "Life" and other magazines once wrote, *"Business more than any other occupation is a continual dealing with the future; it is a continual calculation, an instinctive exercise in foresight."*

Whether you are an entrepreneur, leading edge manager, or a rising star employee; taking time to consider the future, as you may encounter it, is one of the most important activities in which you invest. Your career is important – why not invest in it now! Perhaps you took some time to reflect on your future and that of your team or company over the summer? **Great! So now what?**

- Where do you go from here?
- What changes are you going to initiate to re-invent yourself and ensure what you offer is more attractive and beneficial to your prospective clients?
- What changes are you going to revise in your processes to make them more effective?
- What investments are you going to put into your personal skills training and that of your team?
- What is your 'next' move or 'next' level to strive for?

You see, each of us is continually making changes and decisions which affect our future. I've been quoted as saying, **"The best way to predict the future is to invent it or create it!"** That 'act of creation' is an act of faith and a deliberate *forward thinking* choice we take... we have the opportunity to take personal leadership in making our lives what we imagine and in making the lives of our clients, colleagues, family, and friends better than they ever imagined.

2005: Ever thought... I'm only one person, what can I do?

Ashley and Porsha Demyen were 9 and 11 respectively *(Ashley is standing on the left)*. These two young ladies dramatically answered that question recently when they announced they'd met and surpassed their goal of raising $10,000 for Edmonton's 'Support Network.'

Their goal began last fall when they shared the thought of doing something to put their handprint on the community and caught the vision for helping people who hurt in Edmonton. Their mom works at The Support Network and acted as their assistant, along with their dad. They hand wrote appeal letters and sent them out... the response was amazing... and on April 18th, 2005 *(Ashley's 9th birthday)* they presented a check to **The Support Network** for $10,000.

As I sat in that audience *(quietly wiping the 'wetness' that was leaking from my eyes)* I thought, *"if an 9 and 11 year old can do that... what can I do, what can we as adults do, if we decide to commit and follow through on that commitment?"*

Edmonton's **Bill Comrie** praised their achievement at a recent Support Network fundraising event – **Theresea Comrie Champagne Lunch**, where he was the special guest speaker.

I frequently have people ask me, **"As a motivational speaker... how do you keep motivated?"**

Well, this is one of the ways... being open to the stories of those around me who reach out and move mountains in their lives. Allowing myself to be touched by their stories, moved by their actions and inspired by their personal legends and legacies. We are surrounded by *un-assuming* heroes and inspirational people who simply see a need and decide to do something about it and act on that decision. **Thanks Ashley and Porsha...** you continue to inspire me!

2005: Off to see the world – as an 8-year old adventurer

Off on what would be the 1st of thousands of flights in my life. My dad took a posting in Ventura, CA. working for Goodyear. My sister, my mom, and I flew down when we finished out school year. This was a DC-4 and it took us from Calgary to Los Angeles with only a couple of stops along the way. I think this early flight as an 8-year old sparked my wanderlust.

When I grew up and was able to self-fund, I started travelling the world. When I started speaking and my clients covered the flights, I was overjoyed.

Mom, Bob, and Patti-Robin

We lived in California for a bit and came back to Edmonton for my grade nine year. Coming back to my first winter after winters on the beach was such a shock to my system. **Brrrrrrrrr!** Think that might be why I start planning and plotting to get away when the first snow starts falling.

I believe we can create the life we want to lead... mine is travelling the world encouraging people to live theirs with an occasional stop at the beach. How about you?

2006

2006: The Secret of The Seed!

I moved from New Westminster, BC to the country north east of Edmonton in 2000 for a more creative and casual lifestyle. I traveled the world from there.

When I was home, I frequently had coffee with my 'old' buddy Steve, my 93-year old neighbor, and his two *'younger'* farmer friends, Mike, 79 and Peter, 77. (**2019 update** - Sadly, all three of my coffee buddies have now passed away.) Over the years with them, I learned a lot about farming that is directly applicable to what we do in life and business. I've grown to appreciate the effort and challenges our farmers go through to help feed us. They are amazing, hardworking, and productive people.

Mike and Peter Small rotated their crops based on their *'best guess'* at what will be the best offering in the market for the coming year. They planted canola, wheat, barley, or peas, as selected, each year. When they plant wheat in the spring, they expect to harvest wheat that fall. There is an *'expectation'* that the seeds they plant will produce the crops they expect. They would be very surprised to plant canola and get barley, for example. **The secret of the seed!**

Interestingly, I see people planting seeds for failure and then expecting successful or different results in their business or life. They are surprised when things fail or don't work to their misguided expectations.

Here is the secret of the seed: You get what you plant, nurture, and harvest.

- **Plant the seeds** of creative, personal leadership and responsibility;
- **Plant the seeds** of continuous encouragement, to dream and stretch;
- **Plant the seeds** of equipping your team with the tools and the motivation to win;
- **Plant the seeds** of personal discipline and long-term focus;
- **Plant the seeds** of co-operative innovation and competition;
- **Plant the seeds** of high standards and personal excellence in customer service;
- **Plant the seeds** of creating value-added products and superior services we (*customers*) need; and
- **Harvest** abundance and success at the end of your labours.

2006: As we prepare to move into 2006…

I hope Santa was very good to you and your loved ones last weekend. I enjoyed lots of laughs and meals with my family, extended family, and close friends… and I was definitely spoiled and stuffed.

New Year's is a time when many people make resolutions and some of them even get kept. ☺ I don't make resolutions at New Year's. What I do is revisit my past year and see where I could improve on what I accomplished. I also look at what I had planned and compare that with what I created.

One technique I have used is to visualize myself a year later and ask myself some questions. I find visualization to be a powerful tool. When I was working through the process to attain my professional level **Accredited Speaker** designation, I snuck into the main ballroom late at night and practiced walking across the stage to receive my award. Four years later, (1998) when I did it for real, it was even better than I had originally visualized. I was the 48th person in the world to earn this coveted professional level designation. I had not visualized the sound and the emotion of 2200 plus cheering Toastmasters. It was amazing! (**Update 2019** there are now only 87 who have done so.)

Here are a few samples of the types of questions I use. Fill in the blanks for yourself, add your own power statements and make sure you have these somewhere where you see them on a regular basis.

Looking back on …, I see myself:

- Healthy and in shape with a weight of (? lbs.)
- Productive in my career with an annual salary (commission) of ($?)
- Remembering exciting visits and holidays to (?), (?), and (?) with (?)
- Spending quality, fun and family time with (?)
- Driving my brand new (color, model) (?) with (options) (?)
- Having the satisfaction of completing (?)
- Remembering my excitement of meeting (?) and (?)

- Being able to surprise and spoil (?) with a special (?)
- Being able to say I learned how to (?)
- Meeting my reading goal of (?) books per (?)
- Enjoying the satisfaction of my community involvement in (?) by (?)
- Being recognized for my achievements in (?)
- Meeting (?) and (?) who I have always wanted to meet and asking (?)
- Remembering the many times I shared laughter and love with (?)
- Being able to say, I always wanted to (?) and this year I actually made that dream come true.

I wish you all the success, happiness, earning power, and career potential you can imagine in the following year.

2006: One percent better!

"Excellence results from doing 100 things 1 percent better, rather than one thing 100 percent better." Author Unknown

One of the biggest obstacles to growth is the misguided quest for the big idea, the big break, the big sale, or the big change. However, success, sales, and growth happen one step at a time, one improvement at a time, and often a simple, one percent at a time.

Sure, there are many stories of major breakthroughs and advances, perhaps you've even experienced one or more yourself. However, when you look at what led up to them, you'll often see multiple efforts to improve, research, prepare, and experiment. I know that is often the case in my life and business. I work and prepare in advance of the successful completion or creative breakthrough. It would be so easy, if we could simply wait until the big, million-dollar idea drops into our brains or laps and then reap the benefits. It would also be unrealistic to live that way. It would be like buying a lotto ticket as a means of paying your monthly bills.

Leaders are never fully satisfied with where they or their teams are; they have what many would call *creative discontent* in that they can always see ways of tweaking or making it better. Many of the ones I meet or work with sure live this way. Keeps me on my toes.

Peters and Waterman (In Search of Excellence) wrote, **"*The essence of excellence is the thousand concrete, minute-to-minute actions performed by everyone in an organization to keep a company on its course.*"**

Sam Walton of **Wal-Mart** was *famous* for looking at his competition with the eye of learning *one thing* he could use to make what he and his team did a bit better. He built a large, successful, multi-national company from a very little one by applying this concept of continuous improvement. **Jack Welsh** made some amazing and profitable changes in **GE** by doing the same thing.

My friends at **The Brick** also follow this path to increased success in building a better business and supporting and empowering a better team. Their goal is to create a *'company of leaders'* who will each take increased personal responsibility and creative action to improve their operations and service to their customers.

What are your competitors doing better that you can apply?

I've seen many people fall to the trap of waiting for the *'big idea'* – a completely novel idea for a product, project, or service. They sit and wait for **sudden** inspiration or brilliant flashes of insight. By focusing only on big ideas, we can easily become blinded from seeing smaller, otherwise *'good'* and *'valuable'* solutions.

Like the story I heard of an employee in the **GAP** mailroom who noticed several packages being couriered to the same address. He checked into it, compiled them into one package with instructions on distribution at the receiving end. His *'small'* change in process saved his company tens of thousands of dollars each year.

While not as flashy or showy, these smaller insights and ideas often represent very *workable and profitable* options. Some can even lay the foundation for other great ideas. Encourage your team to capture or share their ideas with you and investigate all the options contained. Consider that the original idea for the one billion dollar a year, **Levi Strauss** Dockers line came from one of their 'dock' workers in Argentina.

Take some time this month to mentally or physically tour your company, to reflect on your career or professional skills.

- **Are there 10-15 areas where you can make changes that will give you a 1% improvement?**
- **Write the ideas for improvement down and schedule specific time to make them happen.**

One percent better can be your rallying call in the pursuit of excellence and success in your leadership, career, or company.

2006: How to handle the 'dream killers' in your life

YOU have this great dream or this fantastic idea bursts into your head. You're excited about the unlimited possibilities and can't wait to share it with your closest friends and family.

What is their reaction? All too often, their initial reaction is to ridicule the idea; to point out its flaws; to remind us about our lack of education, our lack of money, our lack of experience; or to point out how so and so tried it and it didn't work. The result, too often, you let your dreams die, be minimized, or give up on your ideas. **You let your friends and family rob you of your future and your potential for greatness!**

Why do they do that? It might be for a variety of reasons, some of them with the best intentions. It might simply be their concern to see you avoid getting hurt or to sidestep what they see as a path to failure. It may be based on their own fears projected to your action and life. It might be due to a personal failure on their part and a fear that, if you succeed, they will lose you. Or a fear they will have to deal with the reality that, just maybe, they could have done something about their 'seemingly impossible' situation. **Your potential for success scares them.**

How do we handle these 'helpers' or **'idea killers'** in our life? One of the best ways is to be aware of *'their'* existence and seek to avoid them in areas of vulnerability. I don't mean to cut them off completely, just realize that they are not *'committed'* to or understanding of your dreams and desires. Make a conscious choice to keep these areas private, especially during the embryonic or incubation stages of exploring or establishing your dreams and ideas.

Maintain your focus and keep moving forward to seeing your idea or dream become a reality. As someone once wrote, **"Show no regrets for the past, no fear for the future. Expect to win! It's a funny thing in life, if you refuse to accept anything but the best, you often get it."**

We may not choose our family, but we do have full control over the friends we make and over the amount of time we spend with either. This is where we make the decisions that help shape and determine our destiny. In life, there are those who would kill our dreams and those who would, if asked, help nurture our dreams.

We can identify and choose each group in which to associate and invest our time. One of the most effective ways of dealing with an idea killer is in doing your homework. When you have fully researched your dream and have done your due diligence, some can even be brought around to being at least a neutral observer, if not supporter or cheerleader.

Use feedback from these Idea killers as mirrors to reveal your blind spots. They may see things that you might miss in the heat of passion. Keep in mind their input is for **information only** and check it for accuracy before you allow it to impact your decisions.

Demonstrate by your actions; that you're committed to seeing this project through to completion. Demonstrate that you are committed to working on it regardless of the obstacles you may face. Perhaps our past track record of starting and not completing projects influences their support and enthusiasm. This is especially true with *immediate* family members.

Idea killers may occasionally become allies, but it takes massive work on your part to win them over to your team. Keep focused on your Dreams and working with those who are fellow dream builders and cheerleaders! Don't let another person's critical attitude determine your self-worth or your future. You don't know how high or how far you can fly until you spread your wings and take to the sky. Please, don't let another person's limiting beliefs, no matter how well-intentioned, stop you attempting to dream big, to compete for the ultimate prize, achieving your personal dream.

In the mid 80's I belonged to The Entrepreneurs Association. Our Credo was: **"I do not choose to be a common man (or woman). It is my right to be uncommon, if I can. I seek opportunity, not security! I do not wish to be a kept citizen, humbled and dulled by having the state took after me. I want to take the calculated risk, to dream and to build, to fail and to succeed. I refuse to barter incentive for a dole. I prefer the challenges of life to the guaranteed existence; the thrill of fulfillment to the stale calm of utopia.**

I will not trade freedom for beneficence, nor my dignity for a handout. I will NEVER cower before any master, nor bend to any threat. It is my heritage to stand erect, proud and unafraid; to think and act for myself, to enjoy the benefit of my creations and to face the world boldly and say, 'This with God's help, I have done.' All this is what it means to be an Entrepreneur." (*Entrepreneur Magazine was initially our Association publication.*)

This too, could be your credo in being a '*dream builder*' and in encouraging others to build their dreams. This belief is what part of my work as a speaker, trainer, and business coach is grounded on. It is too easy for those around you, who are hopelessly mired in their own mediocrity, to criticize you for trying to follow your dream or acting to implement your great idea.

"Do not follow where the path may lead ... **go instead where there is no path and leave a trail,**" writes an unknown scribe. If you are to receive criticism, and you will, let it be for following your own vision and personal leadership and in daring to build your dreams. Couple that with a sage tip from me, **"Remember, they don't build monuments to critics."**

Good luck in your continued efforts to lead; to build your career, leadership, or business. Don't let the dream killers succeed. **Your success is a beacon to the rest of us who also sail the challenging seas of opportunity.**

2006: Will __? be a year of continued and profitable growth for you and your team?

"Unless you try to do something beyond what you have already mastered, you will never grow." Ronald E. Osborn

When we were young, we were enthusiastic about growing. We wanted to be bigger, faster, smarter, and pursue our dreams. Then we hit the real world and, for some of us, we stopped growing. Perhaps this is where you are stuck, or you see this in members of your team.

Growth is a natural part of life, or it should be. If we stop our growth, then we begin to shrivel and die. That happens in organizations as well. The minute you stop working on the areas that help you grow (recruiting and training staff, marketing and promotion, sales and customer service, business process development, services and products development to name a few) you stop and then start sliding back. The news media are constantly sharing the stories of those organizations which formerly were leaders in their industries now struggling, going down or being liquidated.

Don't let your organization be one of those obits written this year.

How can you avoid this result? It is simple (but not easy) - read on

1. **Invest time with your leadership team** to revisit your goals and performance over the past year. What lessons can you apply from the challenges and mistakes made in the normal process of doing business? When will you apply them?
2. **Work with your complete team** to look at *every facet* of your organization's operations and processes. Where can you make changes to make it easier for your team to win in better serving your customers?

Where can you change your product and service mix to be more accessible and provide for your client's real needs?

3. **Ask your clients to help you.** Ask them to tell you where you did an amazing job serving them and where you need a bit of work. Ask them what you are missing to make their experience better in dealing with you.
4. Ask **what training you need** to be a better leader. Ask what training you need to provide to equip and motivate your co-workers and staff to succeed.
5. What are you doing to **challenge your thinking** and get out of your comfort zone? What books, courses, or meetings are you attending that push you into the winner's zone? Who are you investing time with on a regular basis that challenges you to grow?

These are 5 simple actions you can take in the next few days which will have a dynamic impact on your growth and profitability this year. I challenge you to invest the time to reap the rewards. I wish you, your family, and your team increased success during the upcoming year.

2006: July can be jumping... if you choose

"Our problem with the immediate future will not be the lack of opportunities for the really motivated, but the lack of motivated people ready and able to take advantage of the opportunities." **Buck Rogers (former IBM Leader)**

Summer is an interesting time of year for those of us who are in business or depend upon our ability to promote or sell our services or products. It tends to be a bit slower and *some* people use that as an excuse to cruise or coast and wonder why their year is a bit spotty or lackluster in performance. That can be a waste!

I find this true in many areas: for example, many Toastmasters Clubs close for the summer. If learning to become a great speaker is your goal, doesn't it make sense to work on it all year? Toastmasters is a great place to hone your skills. Even our professional speakers' chapter closes for the summer.

I wonder if working on your business is a strategic decision or not? I miss getting together and learning from visiting experts who come to share with us. Many of my speaker friends also find the summer a great time to work 'on' their businesses instead of 'in' them. I find summer is a great time to enjoy the outdoors, do much needed work outside here in the country, visit with friends, and work on other building or decorating projects left undone during the hectic parts of my year.

I also find this is a great time to do some strategic thinking and revisit my plans and goals for my various business adventures. A great time to catch up on creating new marketing materials, recording clips for the website and podcasts, updating my various websites *(creating new ones and adding a merchant capacity)*, writing ahead on this ezine, completing other writing projects buzzing around in my creative mind *(I can take my laptop camping, on the deck or in the car as I visit friends)* and getting together with fellow speakers, business owners, and professionals to share best practices.

How about you? Summer provides an opportunity to expand your ability to serve your customers and to enhance and add to your own success skills. Use this time to relax and reflect, of course, but use it strategically to add to your professional success and to those you lead. I wish you all the best of summers. Please make sure it is a productive one as well so your fall will be an amazing and profitable time.

2006: *"Don't ask yourself what the world needs; ask yourself what makes you come alive. And then go and do that. Because what the world needs is people who have come alive."* Harold Whitman

This quote was shared by **Renee Perrott**, Valedictorian, Thorhild Central School, Class of 2006 at a recent graduation ceremony. This quote is passionate and very welcome to my ears! *(Thorhild is about 13 km from where I live here in the country, North East of Edmonton, Alberta.)*

As I travel across North America, I hear many decrying the youth of today and complaining about their lack of work ethic or ambition. Frankly, I disagree with that short-sighted negativity! More so, when we are in a great position to engage, educate, and empower those who will succeed us and take care of us in our later years.

*When I talk with the youth of today, I see the **leaders of tomorrow.** I am both inspired and encouraged knowing they are thinking different than my generation. Young people like Renee (18), or Fawn (13) or my student friends at the University of Lethbridge, provide solid evidence that our future will be in good hands.*

We need to have people of passion in leadership roles; people who are not afraid to take risks, to ask the probing questions, to make the necessary changes, and to move us further along the path. I am encouraged that they *'are'* questioning our changing values and are not afraid to challenge the *'beliefs'* of their parents' and grandparents' generations.

Strategic challenge is a good thing; if something is valid and true and retains solid value, it will surmount the challenge. The weaker, non-relevant or non-functional beliefs and systems do not deserve to survive. Truth will both survive and gain strength by being challenged.

In my parent's day, it was typical for people to work for only one, two or maybe three employers in a lifetime. This worked until increased competition and *perhaps* lack of good management and leadership found many looking for employment in the decade before their retirement. This was a wakeup call for their children and their grandchildren, realizing that *blind* dedication to one job or employer was not always a wise move. Employers are learning this lesson the hard way with an increasingly **mobile** labour force.

Today, the majority of the emerging workforce is looking for a challenge, a place to grow and to hone their *portable* skills and talents. They are looking for a better life-work balance and are not as willing to invest *excessive* amounts of time in unproductive jobs or unfulfilling careers. One of the biggest changes is taking time off between jobs. These job gaps are becoming increasingly *less* important in seeking employment as both employers and applicants recognize the changing market has impacted this area too.

Employers are looking for good, solid, creative people who can contribute their energy and expertise. Smart employers are looking for ways to constantly challenge and support them in their quest for growth and value, which might keep them engaged and employed.

I recently read a "study by the Families and Work Institute who polled Generation Y employees and found they were significantly more likely to leave their job than employees who were in their comparable ages in 1977 – 70 percent, compared with 52 percent."

Some *"sock away money for months or give up expensive apartments"* to finance their sabbaticals, but for many, like **Taylor Aikin**, who left a nice job at an architectural firm so he could spend a month biking across the country, the time is right. *"Why now when I'm 28?"* he says. *"Retirement is too far away. And I was too broke in college."* I hear you Taylor... smile!

Amazingly enough, this change is not limited to this age group, as many people in their 40's and 50's are following similar paths. I made a lifestyle choice to move to the country in Northern Alberta in 2000 following the death of my folks in 1999. I downsized and got rid of the second vehicle to allow myself more time for the people and activities I value and enjoy.

I am more selective in the clients I engage and serve. The trade off has been worth it. For the most part, I love it; except when I have a 6:05AM flight! (*I'm a good 90-minute drive from the airport.*)

There are many stages in life. My personal belief is we need to engage each *fully* as we travel through them. We need to be open to change both ourselves and how we interact or connect with our families, colleagues, teams, and our communities. Why not have some fun along the way and make a difference, not just money? Don't get me wrong, earning money is not a bad thing, in itself. I'm not afraid to charge for results. I've increased both my perceived and actual value substantially over the last 5 years, as this allows me more freedom in what I do with my non-billable time.

Let me finish with the wise words of 18-year old, **Renee Perrott,** *"Think of what you stand for. What's important to you? What do you truly believe in? As you leave this stage, think not of what you want to achieve, but about the person you want to be and the way you want to be remembered.* **Let it be something good!**" *Amen to that!*

2006: *"We have adopted a settler's way of life, rather than a thriver's way of life. We settle for good when we desire and deserve great."* Cy Wakeman

If I asked you to do some *honest reflection* on what you've accomplished in your life, your career or your company, what would your answer tell me about where you have '*settled*'? Being a '*settler*' used to have a much different connotation, one of being a pioneer and carving out a livelihood in the harsh, unforgiving wilderness. Not so now! Where have you moved away from being a thriver or pioneer in your efforts, to *settling* for good when **great** is well within your grasp? Where have you *settled* for less than your potential when some '*well meaning*' expert told you couldn't do it?

I am in a wonderful business that allows me to connect with friends, some of whom I've even met, and to grow by that connection. On a recent speaking trip to Iowa I had the opportunity to connect and enjoy the afternoon with **Cy Wakeman** and her family in Sioux City. I went on the NSA site and searched to for professional speakers in the area and emailed the two I found.

One of them, the delightful **Jenny Herrick** was already registered for the District 19 conference. Jenny and I had fun getting to know each other over the weekend. I do that quite frequently, if I know I have any time to spend. If I am going to be in your neighborhood, I'd be happy to have a coffee enroute.

I'll go on the NSA or CAPS or Toastmasters sites and email people in advance. Works around the world and has helped launch friendships in at least 17 countries, so far. I hate *settling* for sitting around hotels and airports when I have the choice to connect with people.

What a great opportunity to share ideas with a productive fellow speaker who moved from being seriously overweight to running and finishing the Chicago marathon in just 18 weeks. WOW! What a great opportunity to sit and chat about life and our amazing business while enjoying the sun and the sound of 11 kids *joyously* playing in the yard *(Cy had some friends who brought their own along)*. What a great afternoon and an opportunity to develop a new friendship instead of just *settling* for sitting in my hotel, again.

During that same weekend I had the opportunity to share a few ideas with three grade eight classes at two different Middle Schools. Some of these talented kids were part of the evening events doing speeches and tackling impromptu table topics. One of these amazing kids was **Fawn** who had the topic *"It's not whether you win or lose, but how you play the game."* Like so many people when given an impromptu question, she proceeded and then stopped, stumped for a minute.

What she did to catch our attention was not sitting down. She did not *settle* for just trying. Instead she took not one but two additional shots at answering this question. I was so impressed at this courageous 13-year old who taught me the meaning of thriving and pushing past the fear. What was even more fun was her mentioning being glad her father was in the audience and pointing at me. Well, she was pointing at the proud father sitting just behind me, as I had been sitting beside her. I cleared up that point during my keynote by saying I would be proud to have a daughter like Fawn.

This speaking and training business does have some unique challenges, in that the travel can sometimes be tedious, and things happen over which you have no control. If you are in sales or travel for your job, you know what I mean. On my way home I had the opportunity to go through Sioux City airport security and board the same twin-engine plane four times due to severe thunderstorms in Minneapolis. Starting with about twenty of us, each time we boarded we had less people who were willing to go. Many *settled* for rebooking and going in the morning.

When we finally left, it was the just the flight crew and me. As I continually told the Sioux City counter staff, *"I'm willing to take the chance, leave my bags on the plane."* I knew when I got to Minneapolis, I had several options. One of them *(which I successfully pursued)* was persuading the airline to accommodate me with a hotel, transportation, and a breakfast voucher. *Been there, done that, got the T-shirt!*

50

That knowledge pushed me past *settling* for the inconvenience due to weather. I used my time in the airport the next morning to do some editing on a book I'm writing, while I waited for the airline to find me a seat. *(PS: I did get home later the next afternoon and Northwest did give me a T-shirt, too.)*

Later that next night, I had the rare privilege of attending a banquet where my friend **Alvin Law**, CSP was the featured speaker. He was one of the reasons I wanted to get home so badly. Even us motivational speakers need a motivational boost at times. Alvin was born without arms and has developed his feet and toes as his hands. Sure, he has challenges, but he did not *settle* for the limitations set by others in where he went to school, the instruments he learned to play *(trombone, piano and drums)*, or stepping up to share his story and challenges with audiences across North America. Alvin has spoken to over 1.5 million students and at least 500,000 adults and finished his first book *(**Alvin's laws of life**)*. I drove home that night, tired, but motivated to move ahead with the challenges in my life. My little inconvenience enroute brought back to a realistic perception.

We can each *settle* for what life deals us, but we can also take personal leadership and responsibility over our lives. I am fortunate to have people like Cy and Alvin in my life along with Kim Yost, Bridgette, Irene and hundreds of others who will not let me settle for being less than my best and pushing past my comfort zone into the winner's zone.

What are you *settling* for? Take a few minutes to think about what you want to accomplish, where you want to go, and who you want to *become* in your life, your career, and your company. Make a concerted commitment to change your direction to one of thriving or pioneering enroute to your greatest potential. Hey, if I can do it, so can you!

2006: March Makes A Difference!

"Only a clear definition of the mission and purpose of the business makes possible clear and realistic objectives. It is the foundation for priorities, strategies, plans, and work assignments. It is the starting point for the design of managerial jobs and, above all, for the design of managerial structures." **Peter Drucker**

- What is driving you and your team?
- What is your defined purpose and strategic mission as an organization?
- What are you doing to engage and motivate your team to win?
- What are you doing to equip yourself and your team to win?

Funny how some non-structured time in the sun with a good book allows your mind to wander and wonder. Amazing how the warmth and sea air can stimulate your imagination and your ability to dream. March is the end of your first quarter and a good time to pause and reflect on how you and/or your team are doing. **Remember those goals you set late last year or early this year?**

I found myself rethinking *'what I do'* and *'why I do it'* on a recent trip to Cancun. I had a wonderful time addressing the dealer/owners of a Canadian National Tire Chain. They were very receptive and open to challenge their own experiences and to revisit *'why'* and *'what'* they were doing. This, I believe, is the beginning of building strong, long-term foundations for profitable success under any organization. I hope my time with them will lead to additional opportunities to serve them and work with their organization. They are a great team of people!

From personal experience, having a *'strongly defined'*, visual image of your purpose and a strategic mission of what you do will keep you focused. It will also keep you fired up and excited about your business and career. It will help you ride the tough times and challenges that come with everyday life and modern-day business. My challenge for you is to take a minute... ok, 15 minutes, and take a serious look at what you are doing.

Ask yourself,

- Why you are doing it?
- What real value do you bring to your industry, market, and clients?
- What are you willing to change to make it better, more attractive, and value-added to your team and your customers?

2006: Change is a conscious 'mental' choice

Sometimes in life, we have pivotal points where we have the opportunity thrust upon us to make changes. A death, a major illness, a sudden storm or typhoon, or a major economic upheaval can force us to take stock of our lives at that point and make needed changes. Isn't it better to seize the opportunities to change and grow as a positive, self-directed choice? Taking control of your life and making positive changes can be both liberating and productive, too.

It is better to be someone open to learn, to stretch, and to push yourself past your comfort zone into the winner's zone. **Jack Welsh**, former CEO of GE led his company through some amazing changes for increased profitability and productivity. He said, **"Change *before* you have to."**

This change is a choice! Life is a series of changes and choices; why not control the direction and pace? Like sailing where you are making a series of changes and adjustments to take full advantage of the wind to reach your destination.

"Searching for the peak performer within yourself has one basic meaning: You recognize yourself as a person who was born, not as a peak performer but as a learner. **With the capacity to grow, change, and reach for the highest possibilities of human nature, you regard yourself as a person in process.** *Not perfect, but a person who keeps asking: What more can I be? What else can I achieve that will benefit me and my company? That will contribute to my family and my community?"* **Charles Garfield**, Peak Performers

Ask yourself a few questions and allow your honest reactions to reflect the changes in your attitudes and actions that need to be addressed to maximize your life and career.

- What do I really want to accomplish in my life? My family life? My career? My business? My community involvement?
- What is my biggest dream? What would be the most fantastic experience?
- What am I afraid of?
- What is stopping me?
- What do I need to change to make it work?
- When will I commit to start making these changes?

Will you have the courage to change? Will you commit to becoming the best you can be, and all that God intended you to become? Remember the words of **J.C. Penney:** *"No one need live a minute longer as he/she is because the creator endowed us with the ability to change ourselves."* The choice is yours!

Success can be as simple as making up your mind to do something or change something and then acting on that change.

2006: *"As we look to the next century (21st), leaders will be those who empower others."* Bill Gates

Personal leadership has become increasingly important in our growth and long-term success. Look behind the scenes of any successful team and you'll likely find a *leader* who has been busy encouraging and empowering their team-mates to stretch and succeed. This may not be a *formal* leadership role, simply someone who cares about the success of their team. It works well in both the business and volunteer sectors.

53

One of the concepts we captured and communicated in **The Brick Way** (published August 2006) was a *serious* commitment from their top leadership to become a *'company of leaders'* where 7000 team members would be encouraged, equipped, and empowered to take increased personal responsibility and leadership for their respective roles. This initial 3-year commitment was reinforced via many different avenues. It drove the growth and success of this great company by tapping into the creative genius of each member; helping them continue to grow and succeed both personally and professionally.

NY Yankees Slugger, **Babe Ruth** once said, *"The way a team plays as a whole determines its success. You may have the greatest bunch of individual stars in the world, but if they don't play together, the club won't be worth a dime."* Talent is not enough, although it is nice to have. Team members who actively work together and support and encourage each other is an amazing thing. Leadership can be the key to team success, and this turns organizations into champions.

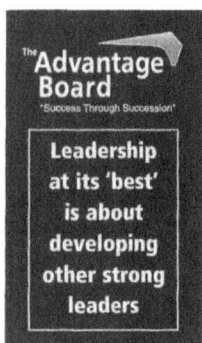

"Every single one of us can do things that no one else can do -- can love things that no one else can love," writes **Barbara Sher**. *"We are like violins. We can be used for doorstops or we can make music. You know what to do."*

Leadership is, in part, about helping your team get the most from their skills and applying those unique skills for maximum success. According to my friend Kim Yost and myself, ***"Leadership at its 'best' is about developing other strong leaders."***

Whether you seek to be a better salesperson, at giving better presentations, or simply at leading your team to greater success, it is great to have people who encourage or support you. I am fortunate to have some pretty amazing people in my corner and it makes a big difference to me. Don't be afraid to ask for help. I have found people willing to help when I asked. At a recent presentation I was asked *"What was the greatest leadership lesson I had learned?"* ***"Asking for help!"*** was what I shared.

- What leadership skills, talents, and creativity can you bring to your team?
- What areas of personal responsibility and leadership remain untapped or unexplored?
- What greatness is within you that has yet to be shared?
- What is stopping you from using them for maximum success?
- How can I help you grow and succeed?

Becoming the leader who you were meant to be opens doors you can hardly imagine. It will stretch you, but the growth will be worth the investment of your time and energy. Your teams will thank you and so will your clients.

2006: Three Keys to Powerful Presentations

In public speaking the cardinal rule to being truly effective is **"NEVER BE BORING!"** But how do we do this when we are nervous and under stress to perform?

Some of you may be thinking, *"Bob, I'm not called on to make presentations."* You may not be called on to make *formal* presentations, but these tips will help you succeed in making better, more powerful client calls, proposals, and informal presentations at work, as well as in your community involvement. Your ability to present well will enhance your career and advance your business success. It will certainly enhance your leadership ability to recruit and work with winning teams.

For the last dozen or so years, I've been teaching leadership clients, fellow speakers, and students my **"three keys to presentation success".** I've shared these tips around the globe. They are based on acquiring the knowledge you need to successfully capture the attention of your audience, connect with them, and achieve your shared or desired objectives. These keys can help you open doors for more effective communication personally and professionally. They can help you equip and motivate your teams to grow and succeed. **Those three presentation success keys are simply:**

- **KNOW your subject or topic**
- **KNOW your audience**
- **KNOW yourself**

If you **know your subject** and are thoroughly prepared, you will be much more relaxed than if you are *'winging'* it. Taking time to organize and delve into your topic will give you a sense of the depth you bring.

It will also give you much more information than you will be able to deliver, which gives you back-up information for additional presentations. This self-confidence based on acquired knowledge works wonders in helping to keep the *'butterflies flying in formation'*, as we say in Toastmasters.

If you **know your audience**, you will be better prepared to effectively analyze their needs and select from the body of knowledge you've acquired on your topic to *better* serve or solve those needs.

The better you know their backgrounds, gender, connections, education, and ages, the more effectively you will be able to construct and deliver your presentation in a way that is both interesting and informative.

If you **know yourself**, you can draw on your own experiences and build on your own strengths to develop your own speaking style. I spoke for **Saputo Foods Limited** and was able to draw on my brief experience in reorganizing a Northern Alberta Dairy Pool distribution dairy in the late 80's. You can also share your own unique stories in a way that allows you to be most effective. Self-knowledge is a tool of effective communication. Being the authentic 'you' can build bridges for effective communication and create increased agreement with your audiences.

Continually ask yourself, **"If I was in this audience, why would I be interested in this point or topic?"** Then simply make sure you have a good answer. Your audiences are people, just like you. The better you know yourself, the better equipped you are to effectively reach them.

By combining and leveraging your knowledge of self, subject, and audience, you will increase your impact. You will also expand your effectiveness as a presenter, interviewee, leader, or speaker. Finally, you will be more adept at helping your audience or your team.

Be sure to apply the **3 P's of professional public speaking - PREPARE, PRACTICE or POLISH, and finally PERFORM!**

There is no substitute for being prepared, by practicing (mentally or vocally) until you are certain you are ready to present your material in a dynamic, interesting, and confident manner.

2006: *"The golden opportunity you are seeking is in yourself. It is not in your environment; it is not in luck or chance, or in the help of others; it is in yourself alone."* **Orison Swett Marden,** *founding publisher of Success Unlimited Magazine*

Happy and smart is the person who stops long enough to both *'see'* and *'seize'* the opportunities that surround them. Each of us has 1440 minutes in our day with which we may capture and/or create magic within our lives and our professional roles. Each day we get up and get out into the world, to explore opportunities to both earn and learn. We also have opportunities to serve and care for our clients which will enhance their lives. Our success is in direct response to how well we act on and leverage those opportunities.

As former IBM leader, **Buck Rogers** said, *"Our problem in the immediate future will not be the lack of opportunities for the really motivated, but the lack of motivated people ready and able to take advantage of the opportunities."* That certainly seems the case here in Alberta with our growing labour shortage and *lackluster* provincial leadership.

Sometimes opportunities present themselves as challenges, obstacles, or problems. The opportunity is seized when a *solution-oriented* mindset is applied. This challenge, when overcome, provides an opportunity for you to grow and expand your skills as well as abilities to serve. It can lead to new products, services, and skills which keep you on the leading edge in your career or business.

Over the past while, I've gotten instruction and coaching in the use of Dreamweaver. This *applied* learning allows me to do some of the little tweaks on my various websites without having to send the materials to Victoria or Mundare and then wait to see it uploaded. The struggle to learn has been an opportunity to expand and leverage my ability to better serve my clients and audiences.

Now, when I have a speaking engagement, I quickly create a special resource webpage just for each client and their respective audience. It has been a great opportunity to dig deep into my creativity. This allows me to create additional value and provide follow up reinforcement to help my audiences act on and leverage my **Ideas At Work!**

I remember my friend Paul, who provided the hosting for our ideaman.net site telling me I should learn to do this many years ago. At the time, I was reluctant *(ok, scared)* to tackle what I considered a major challenge beyond my comfort zone. It was, but it was worth the challenge to gain the skills to better serve and promote my business and services.

Irene Gaudet, from **VitrakCreative.com**, has been patient in teaching me along the way and correcting and tweaking my work. She has been very helpful in helping me create template pages to allow me to do this, as well as helping keep my sites fresh and current. *(Speaking of learning curves, boy, have we been on one in preparing and building the Quantum Success 3-volume series we published this year.)*

- What have you been missing?
- What opportunities are within your grasp?
- What do you need to learn?
- What disguised opportunities await you?

Make this month one of opportunities taken and success will naturally follow.

2006: Sailing Along

*"The wind will keep your sails aloft;
the sun will warm your day; The rain
will help your dreams to bloom and
bring success your way."*

A close friend gave me a lovely little
crystal sailboat trimmed in gold. It sits
on my desk, under my monitor, as I
write this point to ponder. It came with
the above poem, which is very simple,
yet straight to the point. I will cherish it
as I cherish our friendship.

I am now an Albertan, landlocked sailor.
There are model sailboats and other
sailing *collectables* all over my house. In
fact, you'll see a model sailboat to my
left on the desk and a glass case with
nautical knots on the wall.

One of the turning points in my life was my sailing adventure (with the 'baby'
typhoon enroute) from Hawaii to Japan in August 1988. (*I share that story in my
keynote, Against the Wind! www.ideaman.net*)

Although I have not been able to do as much sailing since moving to Alberta, the
salt does run in my veins. Anytime I am near the ocean or see a boat under sail my
heart *still* beats faster. You should have seen me as I walked around the Victoria
harbour early in August.

Do you have something that gets your heart beating faster? What is it? What have
you done to embrace and enhance it?

This four-line poem has all the elements to help us sail along in our quest to
succeed and live a life of significance. Give it some thought as you sail forth to
tackle each day. I wish for each of you the thoughts and best wishes encapsulated
in this poem. Make this month a success. Set sail, trim and adjust them to work
the winds, and set a course for the harbour of your choosing.

I leave you with these words from **Tennyson's poem, Locksley Hall**:

"For I dip into the future, far as the human eye could see. Saw the vision of the world, and all the wonder that could be: Saw the heaven fill with commerce, argosies of magic sails, Pilots of the purple twilight –"

Sail on to greater personal and professional success!

2006: *"The highest reward for a person's work is not what they get for it, but what they become because of it."* John Ruskin

This statement certainly rings true for me in relation to creating and editing this monthly piece of myself for our clients, friends, and our **Ideas At Work!** family.

Amazingly enough, this is our 12th consecutive monthly issue. We published our first **Ideas At Work! e-zine**, in this new format, last May (2005). Next month (May 2006) we move into our second year. Wow! My mom (*a former English teacher*) would *'truly'* have been amazed to see this result. (Update 2019: we published for 10 straight years)

- **I have become** more focused and creative during our time together.
- **I have become** more disciplined in working to deadlines, as well as in advance for the best use of my time.
- **I have become** more observant of the little details that make a difference in my life, my business, and my publications.
- **I have become** inspired and humbled by your responses and positive reaction to what we create and share together each month.
- **I have become** more grateful for the opportunity to serve you, our readers.

Many of you have written or called to tell us where we've been instrumental or inspirational in helping you advance your leadership career or business. Many of you have let me know how an article or idea impacted or inspired you. That makes the effort more than worthwhile.

Bob pictured in a kitchen he designed back in another lifetime.

I'm humbled by your kind words and gracious praise. Thanks!

2007

2007: One more step...

I heard once that **"*Success is measured in inches, not miles.*"** The difference between *'winners'* and *'also rans'* is a single step. In Olympic track events the winner can be a single step, a portion of a second, ahead of the second-place competitor. **Vince Lombardi** is reputed to have said, **"Inches make champions."**

This works in business, leadership, sales, and career races as well. At times we lead by being a step ahead of our competition. At times we lead by taking one more step that *differentiates* us from those who cry, **"ME too!"** At times we lead by taking one more step that brings us in contact with that client who needs what we have to offer and not had the opportunity to hear our story. **Take one more step.**

In sales this is certainly true. Often it is taking that next step to make one more call, one more follow up or sales letter, that makes the difference. It is taking one more step in the direction of your dreams to capture and create the future you desire. It is taking one more *decisive* step that allows you to pull away from the pack and win the business. The same is true in effective leadership.

An amazing friend gave me a collection of sayings. She knows I find this kind of thing intriguing. One of them, by an unknown author is entitled:

"One Step Further"

Do more than exist: live.
Do more than touch: feel.
Do more than look: observe.
Do more than read: absorb.
Do more than hear: listen.
Do more than listen: understand.
Do more than think: reflect.
Do more than just talk: say something.

Made sense to me. This sage advice certainly works in leadership, sales, or business and can have a profound impact on your ability to compete and win. So few of your competitors do more than what is required. They could take the next step, but often they don't.

When things are slow and the sales are stagnant, make one more call, take one more step. **Take it today...** pick up that phone and book the appointment or touch base with a current or past customer.

Remember, out of sight is often out of the running and sometimes out of business. When your team is tired, share one more moment of encouragement with them to take the next step. Take one more step to guide them.

Works in life too. When you have people you love and trust, take one more step to spend time with them. When you are tired and perhaps experience a detour or encounter a pothole in the road of life, take one more step. When you have a dream and want to see it become a reality, take one more step. When you have desires and passions that need expression, take one more step. Sign up for that course, read a new book, listen to a new CD/DVD/Podcast, get a massage, or book that cruise. **Reward or spoil yourself. Do more than live: make a 'leveraged' difference with your life.**

2007: Follow your destiny, wherever it leads you

On the cover it read simply: **"Follow your destiny, wherever it leads you."** The real wisdom was revealed when it was opened. The Blue Mountain Arts card by **Vicki Silvers** began with:

"There comes a time in your life when you realize that if you stand still, you will remain at this point forever. You realize that if you fall and stay down, life will pass you by..." **Vicki Silver's** card went on to state:

"Rather than wondering about or questioning the direction your life has taken, accept the fact that there is a path before you now. Shake off the "why's" and "what if's," and rid yourself of confusion. Whatever was – is in the past. Whatever is – is what's important. The past is a brief reflection. The future is yet to be realized. Today is here."

By now, (Feb) many have made and, sadly, broken resolutions for 2007. That is a process we all encounter. Many will fail to pick themselves up, to dust themselves off, or stiffen their resolve to continue in their quest for self improvement, skills development, and enhanced contribution and value at home, at work, and in their communities. That is sad.

Many of you (*our readers*) will pick yourselves up and are already engaged in moving forward in your life and careers, this year. *I applaud you!*

Suggestion: *I use my birthday as my personal 'new' year and a time to stop, reflect on the year just past, and refocus my energies and intentions for the one to come. I use those intentions as a guide as I dive into each day.* **Remember, today is a great day to start anew.**

A few years back, I spent the day working with CN Rail's Western Region leadership. One of the points we discussed was leaving the 'past' as history and moving on. I reminded them of the old but true adage, **"*Even if you are on the right track, you will be run down if you don't keep moving.*"** It was a very engaging and productive day. Made me think. The Blue Mountain wisdom from **Vicki Silver** was very applicable to companies and their leaders as well as each of us as individuals.

Each year, each month, each day, we each have choices to make in both our direction and our pace. Our choices create our future and our future captures our choices... interesting cycle of success. **When we take personal leadership and responsibility for our lives, we begin the steady process of continual momentum and growth which leads us to succeed.** We begin the process of *leading by example* and converting our lives into *'walking billboards'* of how one person can make a *'leveraged'* difference and make significant progress.

We become search lights shining on the dark, unsubstantiated *'excuses'* others may attempt to hide behind in their own failure to try or grow. We become the encouragers and coaches for growth and long-term success, so sadly needed in our world.

This is our choice. **This is our destiny!** This is the path we follow. This is an exciting time to live!

I am thankful for so many of you who have also chosen to follow this path. Makes for some pleasant conversations along the way and it is nice at times to have someone there to assist if one of us falls or stumbles.

We can bring virtual or in-person support and encouragement for each other this year. This too is our choice to support.

Follow your destiny... better yet, forge your own unique destiny!

2007: *"A customer is the most important visitor on our premises. The customer is not dependent on us – we are dependent on him or her."* **Anonymous**

I'm reminded of these sage words as I relax and reflect in a *quaint* little hotel and spa in Puerto Vallarta, Mexico. I'm sure they could have easily been penned by many Mexican businesspeople, as this attitude is very evident by my hosts.

I am consistently amazed at the open friendliness and genuine attitude of customer service so prevalent everywhere I travel down here. Our hosts and staff seem genuinely glad to see us when we come to eat, get a towel for the beach or pool, ask for a cab to the marina, or ask directions to the local market.

You'd never know that, on average, they make about $8 for a hard day's work. What is it that drives them to be so hospitable while working so hard? It can't be only for the tips, as they were included in the all-inclusive package I booked. You'd never know it from their happy demeanour, even toward the end of a long day working diligently to serve their customers. Their smiles are like a handshake from a close friend. They make you feel genuinely welcome.

Went for a sail (August 21st) on the **Pacific Dreams' Gypsy Spirit**, a 60-foot ketch rigged ship with a crew of three and a couple of helpers from adjacent boats. Oh... yeah... Our host and his crew were very gracious to our needs and even let me take the wheel for most of the trip across the bay to the private little beach at a small fishing village.

Our host took us snorkelling, pointing out the various fish and underwater sites, while the crew prepared an amazing lunch on a beach side grill... way beyond what I would have expected for the price of the trip. Again, a genuine interest in me and in making sure we all had a great day of sailing.

- When was the last time you walked into a store or place of business and had some one lookup and a genuine smile of joy and acceptance cross their face?

- When was the last time you welcomed a customer or colleague in this manner?
- What needs to change to instil this level of interaction and service?

Perhaps we can each learn a lesson, from my Mexican friends, in how to enhance our customers experience with us. Do you think that might help you build your career or business?

2007: *"When we build, let us think that we are building forever. Let it be such work as our descendants will thank us for. And let us think, as we lay stone upon stone, that a time is to come when those stones will be sacred because our hands have touched them."* John Ruskin

Perhaps you have not previously considered your life and your career as a legacy – something you *choose* to leave behind. **The legacy we build,** stone-by-stone, act-by-act, word-by-word, friendship-by-friendship, or client-by-client is our gift to the world and to those who would follow us. That deliberate legacy is our *gift to generations yet unborn*, who will wonder who we were and how we *boldly* did such great things... or not?

What legacy, what gift, do you choose to leave to those you love, to those you lead, to those you serve, or to those who share your passions and activities? Choose to build a positive, productive, and passionate legacy. As you begin your journey into your next year keep these thoughts in mind.

Why not think of that gift (legacy) as something of lasting value? Why not think of it as something that will be an *inspiration* to others who will encounter failures, challenges, or obstacles? People, like you and me, can dust ourselves off, refocus and redirect our energies to successfully move ahead. We can truly lead by example!

- Is it ego to think that we can *live our lives as an inspiration* to others?
- Is it ego to think that *our lives can have an impact* that far survives us?
- Or, is this choice something that is *worthy of our lives?*
- *Can we expend* and invest our energies making sure we *leverage our personal leadership, talents, and skills* for maximum impact and effectiveness?
- Can we do this for the *benefit of thousands* who will hear of us from those who knew us?
- Can we do this *as an example* they can emulate for their own success?

I have chosen to follow the path of **living a legacy** and actively encourage others to do the same. Part of this is a challenge to pass it forward.

People frequently ask me how I find the inspiration to write articles, points to ponder, and so many books. The simple answer is being aware of what happens around me. I look for ideas and concepts to help me share a message of hope, inspiration, and perhaps a few ideas that my readers and audiences can use to build better careers, relationships, businesses, and effective leadership roles. That is my on-going gift to them and to myself.

I wish for each of you an amazing and productive year. A year full of satisfaction, stretching, and service for your clients, colleagues, families, and community. A year of shared laughter and love with those closest to you.

Let me **share a secret** with you... this year can be the most amazing year when you see it as such and build solid foundations beneath that visualization. Build wisely and build to last.

A friend sent this note along yesterday. I include it, in closing, as my wish for you.

"May peace break into your house and may thieves come to steal your debts.
May the pockets of your jeans become a magnet for $100 bills.
May love stick to your face like Vaseline and may laughter assault your lips!
May your clothes smell of success like smoking tires.
May happiness slap you across the face.
May your tears be that of joy.
and... May the problems you had, forget your home address!"

In simple words... May next year be the best year of your life!"

2007: What got you here, won't get you there!

One of the books on my reading list is my friend **Marshall Goldsmith's "What Got You Here Won't Get You There"** with **Mark Reiter.**

Marshall explores why **successful high achievers** have challenges and blind spots that can sabotage otherwise golden careers. Very interesting read and one I am going to dig into as my goal is to continue growing and getting better at what I do and how I perform it. How about you? Are you similarly inclined? Have you encountered challenges in your career?

What caught my attention was one small piece involving research with over 200 high achievers and potential leaders.

These are the caliber of people who could easily jump to another company with even higher compensation. In the survey, each was asked a simple question: "If you stay in this company (present employer), why are you going to stay?"

The top three answers surprised me:

1. **"I am finding meaning and happiness now. The work is exciting, and I love what I am doing."**
2. **"I like the people; they are my friends. This (experience) feels like a team, like a family."**
3. **"I can follow my dreams. This organization is giving me a chance to do what I really want to do in life."**

As you can see the research revealed their answers were never about money. **They were always about happiness, relationships, following dreams, and meaning.**

Wouldn't you love to be able to say that about your current place of employment or role? I would. **Wait a minute... I already do.** ☺

I love what I do! It can be a challenge at times and tiring too; I love every minute of it. I remember telling a Calgary audience at the SOHO business expo that my *intention* is to ***live a leveraged difference***. Each time I help educate, empower, encourage, or otherwise impact a life, organization, or career I extend that leverage. I am privileged to do so. I love this privilege of the platform.

I heard something similar to this at a recent dinner with NSA colleague **Brian Tracy.** The dinner was hosted by my amazing friend **Kim Yost** (who is also a client) and some of his leadership team. One of the team members, let's call him Dale, told Brian why he liked working there and how much he appreciated the chance to grow, to accomplish, and to make a difference. I think Dale *(a great guy and a definite asset on the leadership team)* would enthusiastically echo the words of our survey members above. I love working with this team of *stimulating* characters... Smile! They challenge and inspire me to stretch and grow and I do my best to return the favor. No wonder they lead their industry in Canada. Hmmmm. They certainly make me better!

Brian mentioned he has been teaching some of his ideas for over 25 years... and from firsthand experience that evening they '*still*' excite him. No wonder he is one of our long time NSA Masters. Brian is also very generous with his wisdom and offered to let us use whatever we wanted of his in our **Secret Selling Tips** and other programs. Wow, what generosity!

This addition will increase their value and add a resource to help those who read them. Brian's wisdom spurs me on to grow further in my own career and business. I so appreciate his generosity and willingness to assist me.

Get Marshall's book, **"What Got You Here Won't Get You There"**, apply this wisdom, and be able to look back at an amazing track record of achievement and success that kept growing and impacted other lives for the better.

2007: Powerful intentions

My personal 2007, **"Powerful Intentions"** sits beside me as I write. I carry a copy in my Day-Timer, so I can read it at least once a day while on the road. This keeps them top of mind and helps maintain my *'purposeful'* focus. It also reminds me of personal, higher purpose and goals when temporarily experiencing a *bump* or *detour* along the path.

Create one for yourself. Share it with those you trust and *'Create the Future'* you envision. Then tweak it as you gain a clearer focus of what you want to create in your life, your work, and your relationships.

I have not been sharing mine, other than on a one-to-one basis with members of my informal support and advisory group. **That changes today!**

One of the secrets learned in mastermind or success team experience is the power of accountability, support, and focus. I am enlisting each of you, my readers, in my quest to continue enhancing 'my' world through my work. I believe leadership is best demonstrated by personal example and share these intentions as samples and encouragement to create your own. **Creating one and living it will help you grow and succeed.**

My powerful intentions: Bob 'Idea Man' Hooey – 2007

I have nine points written. Let me share 3 as an example: You'll notice they are written in the *past tense* as though I am looking back on them as accomplishments, as in having achieved them already.

- To *have lived* my life in creating a *'leveraged'* difference in the world!
- To *have been* the friend, coach, cheerleader, and champion for my close friends and colleagues.
- To *have been* a *proactive agent* and dynamic *catalyst for creative change and success* in my world; as well as in all those I touched or influenced via media outreach.

2007: I've been asked on several occasions what motivates me?

Even us *'motivational'* people need a *jumpstart* occasionally. One thing that *inspires* me to keep going, when I am feeling *less* than motivated, are stories of people who have overcome their own challenges and gone on to succeed.

One of them is the dramatic story of a young Oregon woman named **Rachael Scdoris.** I read about her adventures just prior to the 2005 Iditarod Trail Sled Dog Race. Rachael did not finish that year, pulling out after passing the 700-mile mark in consideration for her dogs' health. But that did not dampen her enthusiasm to pursue her dream of completing this race that tests both the will and the strength of its dog teams and their mushers. (*Oh, by the way… Rachael is legally blind.*)

"On March 18th, 2006 at 1:42AM Alaska Standard time, following 12 days, 10 hours and 42 minutes on the trail, 21 year old, legally blind Rachael Scdoris and her visual interpreter, Tim Osmar, passed beneath the wooden structure, known as the Burled Arch, that marks the finish line for the grueling Iditarod. They finished in 56th and 57th place."

Rachael endured the worst that 1,100 miles of the Alaskan wilderness had to throw at her (*temperatures as low as -52 degrees Fahrenheit and wind speeds in excess of 60 miles per hour*) and kept on mushing to place 7th out of the 20 rookies who started the race. Rachael fought for two years to earn the right to compete in the 2005 race and went on to successfully complete it in 2006.

Her dad, **Jerry Scdoris** and I have traded emails over the past year or so. Jerry is, as one would imagine, very proud of his daughter. As he told me, *"For as long as I remember Rachael has talked about running the Iditarod. I didn't take her seriously until she was 15 and she finished a 500-mile race. Now I believe her when she tells me her next goal is to WIN the Iditarod. So, I need to keep working!"*

Rachael's determination caught the attention of people around the world, including myself. In 2005, Nike honored her with the Casey Martin award, established in 2001 to recognize the efforts of an athlete who, like Martin, has overcome physical, mental, societal, or cultural challenges to excel in their sport or who advocates for other athletes who face similar challenges. The award includes a $25,000 Nike grant to the beneficiary of the award recipient's choice.

Last November (2007) in New York, Rachael was named one of Glamour magazine's 10 Women of the Year. Her fellow winners included actress Sandra Bullock, singer Queen Latifah, supermodel Iman, tennis legend Billie Jean King, and American servicewomen.

So, the next time you are having a bad day, your business has a challenge, your sales are a tad slow, or you are just feeling stressed about the challenges in your life, remember this young champion. Dig in, gear up, and mush on. I do! Thanks Rachael!

What makes a champion?

- Is it winning against all odds?
- Is it continuing when others have told you to quit?
- Is it doing your best and giving it your all?
- Is it pushing past your comfort zone into the darkness to learn your limits?

That is the heart of a champion!

- What dangers and fears do you face in your life, in your career, or in building your business?
- What plans have you made to confront them and to tackle them head on?

PS: Rachael is already setting a goal of being a top ten finisher for the 2008 race and eventually wants to be the first to cross the finish line. **Go Rachael, go!**

Note: Over the years while honing my own writing skills, I have had the pleasure of assisting other writers get their ideas into pixels and print. In 2017, we re-organized our **www.SuccessPublications.ca** to offer this service professionally. Check it out.

Follow this link to download a complimentary pdf of this writing resource. **www.ideaman.net/Think.pdf**

2008

2008: *"Efforts and courage are not enough without purpose and direction."* John F. Kennedy

Reflect, Refocus, and Re-commit

2007 is completed and, as they say, in the record books. Whew! Congratulations. You've just finished a very hectic and productive holiday season with work and family activities. Take a deep breath... relax. You worked hard this year, and you've dug deep into your courage, tackle challenging problems and opportunities that crossed your path. But, how did you do living up to your life purpose and in moving in the direction of your dreams?

Reflect! This is a great time to pause and reflect on what you accomplished last year. Are you happy? Are you sad? **Are you amazed?**

- What *could* you have done better?
- Ask yourself, "What you learned this past year that has made you a *better* leader, a better selling professional, or better in your current role?"
- Ask yourself, "What you learned or applied that helped make your community or company a better place?"
- Ask yourself, "What you learned or applied that made your family and relationships stronger, more loving, and more fulfilling?"

Refocus! Set some challenging goals for this year.

What are your goals for this year? What is your BIG, visionary goal for this year? What are your personal goals that impact or enhance your professional ones? What are your goals as a family and how will you work as a team to succeed?

Once you've reflected on last year's achievements and given some serious thought to what you would like to focus on for 2008, take the third step. **Re-commit! Make a personal commitment setting, reaching, and surpassing your goals.**

Write your goals down and put that information where you see it on a regular basis. Share them with your fellow professionals, close friends, family, and, of course, your management team. Ask them to commit to helping you stay focused and positive so you can reach and surpass your goals. All the best! **Make this your best year ever. Visualize it! Write it! Achieve it!**

2008: Where have all the leaders gone? asks Lee Iacocca...

I have just finished reading this very *provocative* and *pleasingly* candid book by a leader who has more than earned the right to speak, and who has no shyness in honestly speaking his mind. Bravo! This is one book that should be on your reading list this summer, along with our **In The Company of Leaders.**

Lee says, ***"The best part of my life these days is my ability to make a difference in the world and to give something back."***

I agree and would take it even further to say, *"The best part of your life (period) is harnessing your abilities and skills to make a difference and to strive to live a life that gives back."* Frankly, that has been my major motivation over the past 10-years and it has been very satisfying to see those **Ideas At Work!**

According to Lee, ***"Leadership is about managing change – whether you are leading a company or a country."*** He outlines his 9 C's needed in leadership. I include them here in point form. Buy his book for the full version and see where they fit in your quest to take increased personal leadership in your own life and career.

- **Curiosity**
- **Creative**
- **Communicate**
- **Character**
- **Courage**
- **Conviction**
- **Charisma**
- **Competent**
- **Common sense**

Lee wrote this provocative book, last year at age 82, as a call to arms for leaders. A much-needed call to arms, I would say. We need more leaders who will step up and claim their place in the world. (buy one soon and read it!)

I love what Lee says later in the book, ***"In a race to determine who will own the twenty-first century, I'll place my bets on the givers, not the takers."*** Amen to that! thanks Lee...

I do have an answer to his question, "Where have all the leaders gone?"

Many of us haven't gone anywhere; we are still here, and we are still working to equip and motivate those we seek to lead in their growth and success. Many of us are working quietly to pass along our insights to emerging leaders and offering guidance and encouragement in their own leadership success growth and paths.

- I've had the privilege of working along-side some amazing leaders in Toastmasters, NSA, CAPS, GSF, and many other organizations over the past two decades.
- I've coached executives from Canada's 50 Best Managed Companies in setting and achieving higher leadership standards and goals.
- I've worked to support leaders who are enduring challenges and helping them assist their teams to more effectively deal with those obstacles to their success.

Each experience has taught me and helped me in my own leadership journey.

On Friday August 15th, 2008 I had the *personal privilege* of sharing from my own leadership insights and experiences with Toastmasters leaders from around the world at their annual International convention, held in Calgary, Alberta.

My **Power of One!** keynote at their annual Leadership Luncheon was to celebrate **'their'** leadership success over the past year. I told them that **'they'** are the answer to Lee's question, "Where have all the leaders gone?"

One very enthusiastic answer is: **to Toastmasters and to their companies, communities, and countries, better equipped to speak up and step up.**

Personal leadership - The Power of One! leads to engaging the passion of many and allows you to walk In the Company of Leaders. I consider myself privileged to walk in their company and yours! Visit: www.SuccessPublications.ca

2008: Thank you, thank you, thank you!

Well, the 2008 Toastmasters International convention in Calgary has come and gone and we have successfully launched **In the Company of Leaders** following my sold out leadership luncheon keynote on Friday, August 15th.

Toastmasters from around the globe are starting to download it. I hope it grows legs and goes around the world, as Toastmasters now has 235,000 members in 141 countries.

I would be delighted if the greater number of them found this e-publication and downloaded it as a tool to help them hone and enhance their leadership skills.

It was great to see a few of our authors in Calgary and to greet 10 fellow Accredited Speakers too.

The Power of One! – leads to engaging the passion of many and allows us to walk In the Company of Leaders. I am honored to be able to walk in the company of these leaders. My thanks to each of our amazing authors whose wisdom made this fly.

"When you speak the audience will listen... When your heart speaks you can capture the world." LaShunda Rundles, 2008 World Champion of Public Speaking

LaShunda emerged as the 2008 World Champion from a field of 10 speakers from around the globe. Her comments provide a lesson for us as leaders as well.

Hearts have spoken and we are capturing the world, one leader and one reader at a time. All the best for the rest of the summer as we confidently move into fall.

Update 2008: I headed south for a much-needed break at the end of the month. Flew to Puerto Vallarta, Mexico Sat (Aug 30th), to do some sailing and generally be a beach bum with a few good books to keep my mind active and recharge. I believe we need to take breaks to recharge, reflect, and refocus. I do attempt to practice what I preach! (Big 'on the beach' smile...) Then I travel back to Edmonton on Sept. 7th for my rappel training that evening. **With your help**, I will be rappelling off the outside of a 27-story building at 9:45AM on Monday, September 8th in support of Easter Seals. Each rappeler must raise a minimum of $1500 to participate. Then I dig back into working on projects and presentations for clients in the fall, including an upcoming speaking trip to Iran, with stop overs in London in November.

Final note:

Being able to keynote in Calgary to a sold out luncheon, being introduced by my friend and fellow Accredited Speaker and International President **Jana Barnhill**, spending time with fellow AS **Sheryl Roush** and **Ross MacKay**, and thanking some of those who helped me grow as a speaker and as a leader, as well as creating and publishing **The Power of One! In the Company of Leaders** allowed me to give back to my Toastmasters family... **this was a rare privilege,** and one I did not take lightly. It has been an amazing summer and I look forward to an even more amazing fall. (**Update 2019**: we did a 95th anniversary edition.)

2008: *"It is not death that a man should fear, but he should fear never beginning to live."* **Marcus Aurelius**

Lost another good friend late last month, 2008. *"He simply went to bed and forgot to wake up,"* as my 95- year old buddy Steve told me.

When we suffer the loss of someone close to us, it cannot but impact us on a deeper level. Certainly, a time to pause to ponder and to reflect on their contributions to our life. Someone once told me, **"When someone dies, we are diminished in some way by their loss."**

I suppose that is true, but we retain a part of them in our memories, in our minds, and in our message as impacted by their interaction in our lives. Peter was an important part of my life. His cousin, **Dan Small**, spoke briefly about his life and shared some of the stories from earlier years.

Peter Small was many things: a son, a brother, an uncle, a cousin, a hard worker, a mechanic, an inventor, an innovative farmer, and a philosopher ("it will be better, next year"), plus a real friend to many of us. I had the privilege of his friendship over the years, since I moved out into the county northeast of Edmonton, Alberta. **I will miss his kind spirit, his gentle personality and mischievous sense of humor, his hard-won words of wisdom, and his genuine soul and smile in my life.**

Peter was a founding member of the **Egremont Bachelors Club,** of which I was a junior member. I have often told folks as I travel to speak across North America, that *"I am the young, studdly one."* PAUSE, *"OK, the young one!"* I go on to explain our membership consisted of Steve (95), Mike (80), Peter (78) and myself. This usually garnered a chuckle or two.

74

Mike and/or Peter faithfully came every day *(unless they were away or working in the fields)* to pick up Steve for lunch and again for coffee about mid-afternoon. I would often join them for a coffee break, when I was up to my eyeballs in a project or prepping for a presentation. I loved being able to discuss the world's challenges with these warm hearted, wise men, and anyone else who would join us. I also loved being able to share my travels, travails, and occasional triumphs with my friends. **But now there are three...**

I share this with you because life is short, even for those in their 70's, 80's, or 90's. **We need to embrace life; not just exist, to face each challenge, and to stretch ourselves to our fullest. Life is an adventure to be lived to the fullest; each day is a gift (that is why it is called the present.)**

My challenge for each of you is to live your life to the fullest, to leverage your abilities and skills, and to leave a rich legacy for those who follow. **My friend Peter did!**

2008: Impressions of Iran

I recently completed a speaking tour of Iran where I spoke to a variety of audiences (6 days in a row). One of the most asked questions during my 8 days in Iran was, **"What are your impressions of Iran?"** Followed by, **"When will you come back?"** I was even asked these two questions during my interview on their national TV.

Quite simply I told them, "I came with no real expectations other than comments from some of my speaker friends of being well treated on their visits. I wanted to experience *you* for myself. What I experienced first-hand was wonderful people with warm hearts who accepted me and my ideas. Wonderful people who were so hospitable."

I told them, *"You are amazing! I have never been so welcomed or well treated in my travels. The world needs to know that the Iranian people are wonderful."* And in answer to the second question, *"When someone invites me back."*

The Iranians loved our little **Pocket Wisdom** series. I had the distinct privilege to share my ideas both on stage and off with a variety of audiences. Fortunately, I had an amazing translator who helped me convey my ideas. Thanks again, Sepehr!

On Sunday (November 9th), I shared some ideas with forty or so branch managers from Iran's largest distribution company to assist them in getting ready for a major product launch later that month. I saw their Managing Director later in the week and he was expressive in his thanks for really helping him.

On Monday afternoon, I keynoted the third annual Strategic Management conference and shared some ideas on personal leadership. I closed with an Iranian saying, *"May peace be upon us"* and may our leadership bring about this peace in our lives and our countries. I was overwhelmed when the entire audience stood and started singing back to me. I was later told they were responding to my comment about peace.

On Tuesday, I spent the entire day with 170 sales managers from around Iran with the Industrial Management Organization.

They had run ¼ page color ads in the local paper as well as articles. During the break I noticed people picking up papers and the second section had an article with my picture on it. how cool was that!

We also had our first Iranian sign ups for our **Secret Selling Tips** and our upcoming **Secret Leadership Tips,** which moved us from being a North American company to an International one.

Later that week I received a personalized Waterman (Paris) pen and this note from a Managing Director who had his team attend that session:

"Dear Mr. Hooey: *Thank you for* **elevating my Sales Team's knowledge during your sales management seminar** *in Tehran (Iran). I look forward to meeting you in person during your future seminars. Warm regards."* **Mendi Ghaemi**, Managing Director, Bidar Group, Tehran, Iran

On Wednesday and Thursday, I spoke at Sepehr's Time, Stress & Memory Management conference along with **Kevin Kelly** (from Ireland) and **David Thomas** (from England) to a sold-out audience of over 550 people. We were mobbed when we were off stage by people eager to share their experiences and to thank us for coming. Wow!

Thursday evening, Sepehr (our client and translator extraordinary), David and I boarded a very old plane to fly to the Island of Kish (in the Persian Gulf not too far from Dubaï) where we would speak **Friday** at the Kish International Campus of the University of Iran to a group of 200 plus energetic students, faculty, and business leaders.

They cancelled all their classes so the students could attend our sessions at this special conference. They put together the conference just to take advantage of David and myself being in the country. It was confirmed just a week before we flew into Tehran.

Bob pictured here with Sepehr Tarverdian while speaking in South Africa

I was again *overwhelmed* by the warmth of their response both on and off the stage (picture above is audience asking questions following my first session) to my two messages on personal leadership and productivity (or time management). I was further humbled by the kind words of their dean, included here:

"Dear Bob Hooey: *It's a great pleasure and an honor for me to have hosted you in our conference in November 2008, in the beautiful Kish Island.* **Your shared insights and practical tips have enriched our understanding of the current tough business environment and life.** *I once again express our heart-felt gratitude and thanks to you, for having accepted our invitation to speak in our conference. May you prosper in every endeavor you undertake in your life in the future.*"
Dr. Nosratollah Zargham, Head of Kish International Campus, University of Tehran.

Saturday, my young friend and delightful guide from our week, **Sogand Sedighi** *(pictured here)* who is currently working on her MBA, teaches English, and is married to a professor, picked me up at the hotel and took me shopping for the afternoon.

With her wise help, I was able to purchase some very nice scarves, jewelry, and other Iranian mementos to bring home with me.

I was also able to collect some coins and older (out of circulation) bills for my friend **Kim Yost** who collects them. He was ecstatic when I gave them to him upon my return.

Saturday evening my friend, Sepehr came to the hotel to spend the evening and brought along an amazing, beautiful, silk, hand-woven Persian rug as a wedding present for Irene and myself. It catches your eye as you enter my office!

It was a bit of a challenge getting it safely home, but Irene and I will cherish his generosity of spirit and his wonderful gift. Then I flew to London on Sunday morning, where I spent 4 days playing tourist in London before returning home.

2008: "Home is where the heart is..."

Or, so I have heard in the past. Following a recent trip to Iran, with 4 days in London on the way home, I have a much better understanding of this comment.

Irene and I were recently married (Las Vegas on Oct 4th, 2008). I am truly blessed to have her in my life. We make a great partnership in life and in business, and she likes to travel and sail... how lucky can one man be!

Normally when I travel, I am not *homesick*, however this last trip was different. Despite an amazing reception in Iran and some interesting sites in London, I found myself missing her more than usual.

We were able to Skype via the computer and would talk almost every day, which helped a lot. I couldn't help wishing she was there on occasion to share the experiences, especially in London (Irene has been there before and told me lots of places to visit.)

Amazing how things change when you make a commitment. Now this may seem funny coming from me, as I have wished Irene was along on some of my other trips, but this time it was more obvious to me.

It just *crystallized* how important it is for me (and I hope for you) to keep connected with those we love, and with those who we hold important in our lives. This is one of the reasons I do this e-zine every month, even when my schedule is, at times, hectic. I hear from so many of you that you enjoy reading it, enjoy hearing about my *little* adventures, and on occasion you share where I have been able to inspire or challenge you to grow. I even have several family members, including my sister, who subscribe *just* to keep an eye on me. Smile!

That keeps me focused and working on your behalf. I miss you too, when I travel. I also have the amazing privilege to add new friends and extended family as I travel the world, and this is one way to keep in touch with them as well.

2008: Give the gift of inspiration

Ever thought, **"I'd love to be able to be an inspiration, but I'm just a _____"?**

Wanted to give you something to think about as you begin your year. How can you make the lives of those you serve, work with, live with, or come in contact on a regular basis, better, more fun, and perhaps even changed?

My friend **Barbara Glanz** is like that for me. We've been friends and colleagues now for close to 20 years. I don't see her that often, usually at an NSA event. But she makes me feel special and I love her for that.

- Who do you make feel special?
- Who makes you feel special?
- Have you told them thanks?

Pick up a phone and call them!

2008: Plan your work and work your plan

No doubt you've heard this statement in the past and perhaps it sounds like a bit of a *cliché* from overuse? It has within it a kernel of wisdom and truth that we can use to productively and successfully grow our businesses, our careers, our sales volumes, and even our relationships.

I have lived in the country northeast of Edmonton, AB for almost 8 years (**Update 2019**: 20 plus years) and each year I plan to improve something here. Might be painting the garage, creating a writing room, rebuilding my fences, creating a walking path to my neighbors, adding to one of the decks, or adding a new flower bed.

This year I decided to take a raised area along my driveway, currently grass with a small flower bed, and convert it to a rock garden. Plans include planting flowering fruit trees, additional bushes, perennials, and spots for attractive annuals to add color to this area. There will be a double trellis, bench seating, and a foot path to the middle of this area with the insights and expert help of my gardening diva, Irene.

That is the plan. The implementation of that plan has taken a bit longer than I had thought due to rain and an extremely dense, packed area to be dug up. It is coming nicely. We will have the trees and some of the perennials in this year for sure, but the finished product might take until next year. Will it be worth it? Of course, but it takes work. Doesn't everything look good!

Being successful in your leadership role, your career, building your company, or enhancing your sales takes similar effort. A good plan (vision), built-in flexibility (adapting to change), a commitment to turning over the sod (or fill in the _____), cultivating the area and soil (relationships), planting, and, of course, watering (marketing and other investments) until you see the growth or completion you originally envisioned.

I wish for each of you a great summer. Take some time to reflect and refresh yourselves and plant seeds of success in your lives and involvements.

2008: *"We shall fight on the beaches, we shall fight on the landing grounds, we shall fight in the fields and in the streets, we shall fight in the hills; we shall never surrender..."* Winston Churchill

Have you ever suffered a set-back, defeat, or been stuck on a detour in your career, company, or community involvements? Have you ever had one of those days when you felt just a bit disillusioned and down? Have you ever felt like you were alone in your battles and wanted to throw in the towel?

I have and I'm sure everyone who has achieved any level of success has gone through several *dark seasons of the soul* enroute to their success. My friend **Michel Neray** and I chatted about this... He said, *"Sometimes the hardest thing is to figure out whether you are doing the wrong thing and that's why you're not getting the result you want, or you're doing the right thing and you simply have to give it more time. There's no guru or simple formula to help you figure it out – you just have to let your heart, head, and gut battle it out, and then do whatever wins out."*

Taking inspiration from someone who has experienced seemingly overwhelming odds might provide a small inspiration in your situation. For example:

The date was June 4th, 1940 (68 years ago) and it was *painfully* clear that France was about to collapse under the military might of Nazi Germany. There was still an Anglo-French alliance, of sorts. The United States was *still* keeping its neutrality and it was obvious that Britain stood, to all intents and purpose, alone. How would you like to deal with that less than 3 weeks after being given this leadership role following the resignation of Prime Minister Chamberlain on May 10th, 1940?

This is exactly the situation **Sir Winston Churchill** took on and this famous quote was from his June 4th speech delivered in the House of Commons to gain their support and to rally the support of the British people.

81

He did not *gloss* over the challenges or the strength of their enemy; in fact, he was more than accurate concerning their abilities and their intent. He did however speak to the soul and the commitment to fight this enemy for how ever long it took.

- How *solid* is your commitment to your growth, your career, and your success?
- How *committed* are you to fighting through and giving it what ever it takes to reach your goals and to see your ideas become reality?
- How *committed* are you to dealing with the challenges enroute to proving to yourself, your family, and your friends that you have what it takes to be a winner?

Here is the quote in its full context:

"Even though large tracts of Europe and many old and famous states have fallen or may fall into the grip of the Gestapo and all the odious apparatus of Nazi rule, we shall not flag or fail.

*"**We shall go on to the end**, we shall fight in France, we shall fight on the seas and oceans, we shall fight with growing confidence and growing strength in the air, we shall defend our Island, whatever the cost may be, **we shall fight on the beaches**, we shall fight on the landing grounds, we shall fight in the fields and in the streets, we shall fight in the hills; we shall never surrender, and even if, which I do not for a moment believe, this Island or a large part of it were subjugated and starving, then our Empire beyond the seas, armed and guarded by the British Fleet would carry on the struggle, until, in God's good time, the New World, with all its power and might, steps forth to the rescue and the liberation of the Old."*

And fight they did and they won. You can too! Take a fresh look at the challenges you face and dig deep into your courage and conviction to fight again and to win.

2008: "Who are the happiest people on earth?"

"A craftsman or artist whistling over a job well done. A child building sandcastles. A mother, after a busy day, bathing her baby. A doctor who has finished a difficult and dangerous operation and saved a human life. Happiness lies in a constructive job well done. Get your happiness out of your work or you will never know what happiness is." **Elbert Hubbard**

March is a month for personal motivation. For many of us in business, March is the end of first quarter of the year. March is a great time to pause, reflect, and revise what you have been doing.

March is also a great time to pause, refresh, and push ahead on those critical, constructive projects and activities which move your career or business to a more productive level.

March is a time to make sure you are doing what you love, something that brings a sense of satisfaction, feeds your passion, and, yes, even adds happiness to your life. Nothing is tougher than working in a role or for a company that saps your energy, devalues your contribution, or ignores your potential.

A wise man once told me, *"If you love what you do, you'll never work another day in your life."* After a decade and a bit, working as a motivational speaker, sales and leadership writer, business success coach, and inspirational author, I am beginning to understand what he meant. I love what I do and the chance to leverage my learning to help other folks. I love the feedback I get from our readers and audience members as to how we have been able to encourage or equip them to make positive changes and reap profitable results. That keeps me going and feeds my passion.

That is not to say I don't work at it or even struggle at times. Any business has times of challenge and change that impact our day-to-day motivation. I have endured periods where I truly wondered about the wisdom of choosing this path, like the period following 9-11. I have disciplined myself to stay the course, to keep pushing, to keep working, to keep writing, to keep speaking, and to keep believing in what I offer to the world. You can too!

If you are not working in a role you love, look for ways to change it to be more reflective of what you want and value in life. If that doesn't work, then give serious thought to brushing off your resume and look for a place that fits and allows you to grow. If that doesn't work for the short term, look for community activities that feed your soul and give you an enhanced sense of purpose. Life is too short to labor while undervaluing yourself, your gifts, and your expertise.

Make March a motivational month. Move ahead with productive activities and involvements that make sense to you and make you a happier person. You'll be glad you did and so will everyone around you.

2008: Point to Ponder

Observing and measuring performance - Keys to effective coaching
If you are truly dedicated to helping those you lead or supervise to improve their performance and productivity, it helps to carefully watch them in action.

Professional coaches in the athletic arena use on-site observation and film replays. This allows them to isolate and work on specific areas, techniques, or skills needing work.

In the business world these *'instant replays'* may be filtered or edited by the people reporting them to the coach/manager/leader. It is difficult to know how well people are doing without observing and/or tracking their performance.

Better observation systems and relevant information will lead to a better result and better coaching.

Over the years, one of my bigger management challenges was to work with those whom I supervised to be more productive on the job. I've had a fair amount of challenge and success as a small business owner and as a manager for larger firms in helping my employees succeed. **I just love it when people grow and win!**

Long before coaching became a 'buzz' word, I found myself using some of these *'management'* techniques coaching my staff, helping them set goals for successful learning, and moving their skill sets up the ladder so they could be promoted. In the 1970's I was hired to open a Big Boy's franchise in Edmonton Center. A year or so later, I was asked to go to Calgary and assist the franchiser there in re-energizing his staff at 3 stores. After my departure, my two assistants were promoted; one to take over my store and the second to take over the store in the east side of the city. Their leadership skills had been honed and they had the chance to shine. They each did very well.

I had a similar experience when I was *head hunted* as part of the management team to open the first Home Depot in BC. Several of my staff were tapped to move up into management as new stores opened. I have found that coaching as part of the training and motivational process works very well.

It works well in the management of volunteers too. I could tell you many success stories of boards and those who responded well to these leadership coaching techniques.

One example was during my extended term as President of CAPS-BC, (1999 & 2000). We had a serious *organizational* challenge as we had a low bank balance, low membership, and low energy in our meetings. It took recruiting and creating a motivated, success focused executive team to make it happen and to reverse the process. It took a leadership coach to call the plays, help set the goals, and continue helping our volunteer leaders grow to take on their respective roles and to serve our membership. **Did it work?** You bet it did!

At the end of our extended term, we had tripled our membership, had a healthy bank account, a reasonable budget for the next year, a 3-year succession of leaders (succeeding presidents did an awesome job), hosted the following national convention, a healthy fully-active board, the next year's meetings already booked, and a very *relieved* and *tired* Immediate Past President.

Canadian Association of Professional Speakers National recognized our growth in 2000 by awarding us Chapter of the Year and our CAPS National President, Patricia Katz awarded me a special CAPS President's Award **'for my energetic contribution to the advancement of CAPS and my living example of the power of one'**. I was overwhelmed at this recognition, as I did not see it coming. Yes, Coaching works!

Successful managers (coaches) look at both the results and the process to find areas where they can assist their employee's or member's fine tune or tweak their success skills for enhanced performance and productivity.

Performance observation and measurements must be done on a regular, recurring basis to offer ongoing validity in your coaching efforts. A little feedback and instruction closer to the activity is the most effective. Performance reviews, as done in most businesses once or twice a year, are not effective and can at times be counterproductive.

Learning how to observe your employees or team members without making them feel intimidated or uncomfortable is a skill you'll need to acquire as you evolve your leadership and coaching expertise.

2008: *Listen to that voice inside you that says you can accomplish anything. Trust that feeling that tells you, you can achieve all that you hope for. Believe that everything you want is waiting for you. Hold on to the knowledge that nothing is impossible. Remember that each person who has ever achieved a goal started out with only a dream."* Jason Blume

Have you ever felt your spirit nudge you?
Did you respond or did you tell yourself to grow up and deal with the facts?
Did your fear stop you from moving?

Our intuition is an important part of our life and like other skills it can be nourished and honed. Try it on smaller nudges and check it out; then confidently move ahead to let your spirit lead you to greater success in life and business.

Life is much too short to live in doubt, to struggle needlessly, or to undervalue your own skills, experience, or expertise. Dream on and make those dreams come alive!

Ask those who have struggled and overcame obstacles to succeed:

- They will tell you that they believed in themselves, despite the obstacles.
- They will tell you that they believed they would emerge victorious, and they worked to make that belief a reality.
- They would tell you it was worth the struggle.

I travelled to **Tehran, Iran** and I am confident that this trip was beneficial for those in my various audiences as it was profitable for me as well. One of the groups I addressed was composed of 150 Sales Managers from the middle east who were be given the opportunity to join our Secret Selling Tips subscribers.

I told one of my audiences that there was increased talk of a recession and **"I had decided not to participate."** In fact, I told them I was working to make this challenging time one of my most productive.

In times of challenge, people need help. They also need hope. **That is my business!** I can give them a hand with both these areas. Let me challenge you to listen again to your voice and then move confidently in the direction of your dreams.

2008: Does one life make a difference?

This was the 'title' of my original Accredited Speaker audition presentation for entry into the Toastmasters International professional level program back in the mid 90's. It explored the concept that each of us *already* makes a difference by our choices, our actions, and our interactions with those around us – the choice was in what kind of difference (Positive or Negative). The judges passed me, and I was accepted into the program. I went on to earn my Accredited Speaker designation in August of 1998 in Palm Dessert. **Does your life make a positive difference?** I trust it does!

August 15th of this year (2008), I had the *rare* privilege of keynoting the Toastmasters International annual leadership lunch at their Calgary convention. My keynote laid out the contention that Personal Leadership tapped into **The Power of One** which leads to engaging the passion of many and allows us to walk **In the Company of Leaders**.

I further challenged those in attendance to step up and claim their leadership – that the world needed their willingness to lead and to make a positive difference.

On September 8th, I joined 62 fellow Edmontonian in support of Alberta Easter Seals and stepped off the ledge of the 29 story Sutton Place Hotel as part of the 2008 Edmonton Drop Zone adventure.

Together, my fellow Superheroes and those who supported us, we raised $98,730 to help adults and kids with disabilities here in Alberta. Across Canada other superheroes stepped up to do the same thing in their cities.

As I mentioned at the celebration dinner honoring my fellow Superheroes, "It takes personal leadership to do what we just did, to confront our fears and step up and step out. When we do that, we become leaders, role models and we inspire others to follow in our footsteps... although perhaps they don't realize how far they will step." *Picture is me on the ledge 29 stories above 101st St... gulp*

I went on to mention, "When I travel the globe talking about effective leadership, I remind audiences about the *ripple effect* of their personal leadership. One great example is my friend **Catherine Vu**. Catherine heard about my Drop Zone adventure last year and told me she was going to do it and recruit a team. Well, she did!

"She invited a few friends, who invited a few friends, and they created the Drop Zone Daredevils (9 people who raised in excess of $20,000). Each of us can inspire others to individual and team greatness. Each of us can be a leader, and the world desperately needs more leaders and superheroes."

Superheroes are *ordinary* people who step up when needed and sometimes step out in support of their respective causes.

Thinking back over the past 17 plus years, I have seen a thread woven in my remarks that I trust has been worn in my actions and intentions. My icebreaker speech for Toastmasters (First one back in 1991) was called **'One Small Candle'** which contrasted the funerals of a young person taken early and an older person who had lived a rich life of service and significance.

I shared with that audience of very supportive Toastmasters that my *intention* was to live my life in such a way that it would make a *significant* difference.

When the next election happens, get organized and get out the vote. Our respective countries are crying out for **strong, effective, leadership** and that starts with us. You and I can make a difference by living our lives in such a way that we inspire those around us to greater action and success.

And, of course, get out to vote. My neighbor Steve (he will be 96 next month) was one of those who went to fight in WWII leaving behind a young son and wife. My dad and uncle both served in the Royal Canadian Air Force, in service to this country and in support of democracy. Our vote is a remembrance of their willingness to risk their lives and the sacrifice of thousands who died to ensure our freedom of choice. We stop to remember them on November 11th; but we can ensure their memory is preserved each time we *exercise* what they fought to support – **freedom to choose, freedom to lead, freedom to live, freedom to make a significant difference! And you can...**

2008: Point to Ponder
"Whatever you can do or dream you can... begin it. Boldness has genius, power, and magic in it." Goethe

When things are a bit rough or the going gets tough, it can difficult to believe in your dreams, to resist the urge to pull back and not pull your head down. I understand that from firsthand experience.

However, when things are going tough, it may just be a blessing in disguise. Now, some of you may think I'm losing it when I say that, but I do believe we get gifts given to us in disguise. Often, they come in work clothes and the gift is only discovered after they have been engaged.

When things are tough, we get challenged to re-evaluate our lives, our careers, and our involvements. We get to choose what is important to us and where we will invest our limited time and resources. This can help us clear out less important or distracting activities or commitments that hold us back from our long-term passion and success. We get the chance to re-evaluate our business and career choices and perhaps make changes that we would not make if still in our comfort zones. We get the opportunity to discover the true friends and supporters in our lives and to be there for those we care about. **The greatest gifts** or assets in our lives are the people with whom we connect and build relationships.

It is our connection with people that helps to open doors, sharpen our skills, and lead us to greater accomplishments. I am truly blessed with the amazing people I have in my life and my various roles.

I am especially blessed with my wife Irene who walks beside me and is a source of encouragement. Each month I have the privilege of sharing a few thoughts and ideas with you. That too is a blessing in my life.

"Don't put limits on yourself. So many dreams are waiting to be realized. Decisions are too important to leave to chance. Reach for your peak, your goal, your prize. Realize that it is never too late. Do ordinary things in an extra-ordinary way. Have health and hope and happiness. Take time to wish upon a star." **Colin McCarty.**

2008: The Three Most Common Training Mistakes
You're probably making at least one of them now!

As an owner, manager or team leader, you may frequently make decisions to engage or contract on programs and policies that will either help or hinder your team in reaching their goals.

Unfortunately, training dollars will ultimately be wasted whenever leaders make some of the following mistakes.

Here are the more common ones to consider:
   1) Failing to fully assess team needs.
   2) Thinking (wishfully) that training sessions will eliminate conflict.
   3) Thinking of training as a program vs. a process.

You can avoid making training mistakes by considering a few ideas, and side stepping some mistakes that, for others, have minimized returns on their training dollars.

I include this article in our September issue, as that is when many companies ramp up their training. **Training can and should be a big investment in your future success. Training needs to be focused and effective.** I want to challenge you and perhaps nudge you a bit in making sure your training pays off for you and for your team. I'd love to help if I can!

Update 2019: I shared these tips at the 12th annual HR summit in Manila in August.

2008: Kraft Dinner – now you're cooking!

The story behind this decade-by-decade best-seller, as I learned it, happened following the war when **Kraft Foods** had pallets of their powered cheese packages (used by servicemen during the war) sitting 'unsold' in warehouses across the country. One particular east-coast manager was 'actually' selling out and headquarters sent someone to find out his secret.

As I heard the story, he creatively took the powered cheese packages, bundled each with a package of pasta and called it **Kraft Dinner**. Love the story and the creativity behind it. What do you have and what can you combine with it to make it more attractive or appetising to your clients?

Creativity is a leadership and business success tool. Hone yours to grow!

2008: There is a difference between training and education.

Both have their place, and both are important.

I was shopping in a retail store the other day and put my purchases and a $20 bill on top on the conveyor belt. The very nice lady behind the till took my $20 off and put it to the side. She then proceeded to ask me, **"Will this be on your _____ card or debit?"** With a straight face, I said, **"No thanks, Cash!"**

She had obviously been trained to say that, but not educated as to when it would be appropriate. When you are training someone, please ensure they are educated at the same time.

This was me when we opened Aikenheads which was bought by Home Depot before we even opened our doors to the public.

I have a fair amount of experience in retail and teach that actively listening vs reacting to our clients is a success skill.

90

2008: Egremont speaker joins 63 local superheroes to raise $98,730 for Alberta Easter Seals

"Being a superhero is really about facing your fears and stepping up." On Monday, Sept 8th it was about stepping out – backwards from a ledge 29 stories above a busy intersection in downtown Edmonton. Trusting the gear and the support team, local speaker and writer Bob 'Idea Man' Hooey did just that, dressed in the 'Old TV Batman' costume for Alberta Seals 3rd annual Edmonton Drop Zone. Each of them rappelled 29 stories down the outside of Edmonton's Sutton Place Hotel.

This is Bob resting (slumped) against the wall following a successful rappel last year. Bob hopes it will be less terrifying and less of an emotional challenge this year...whew!

Bob admits to being very afraid of heights but is committed to helping Alberta Easter Seals raise needed funds for adults, kids and seniors with disabilities. Alberta Easter Seals helps them with needed equipment to allow them to enjoy a more normal quality of life. His commitment helped him work through his fear.

As Bob said at the celebration dinner honoring the 63 local Superheroes, "It takes personal leadership to do what we just did, to confront our fears and step up and step out. When we do that, we become leaders, role models and we inspire others to follow in our footsteps... although perhaps they don't realize how far they will step."

He went on to mention, "When I travel the globe talking about personal leadership, I talk about the ripple effect of that personal leadership. One great example is my friend **Catherine Wu**. Catherine heard about my Drop Zone adventure last year and told me she was going to do it and recruit a team. Well, she did! She invited a few friends, who invited a few friends and they created the Drop Zone Daredevils (9 people who raised in excess of $20,000).

"Each of us can inspire others to individual and team greatness. Each of us can be a leader, and the world desperately needs more leaders and superheroes."

Bob gave copies of his new e-book, **"In the Company of Leaders"** to each of the Superheroes and copies will be sent to each superhero across Canada as a thank you for those who stepped up in the various cities across Canada with Drop Zone events.

This was the 3rd year for the Easter Seals Drop Zone in Edmonton and substantially the most successful with more than double the superheroes who raised more this year than the previous two years combined. All it took as a few people to screw up their courage, ask for support, and step out and off for a great cause.

Looking back, I see subtle changes in myself, in how I look, how I act and how I think! Most of them snuck up on me while I was busy working on a project or struggling with a challenge or difficult decision. Hmmm

I hope you enjoy The early years (1998-2009) and continue on to read The saga continues (2010-2019)

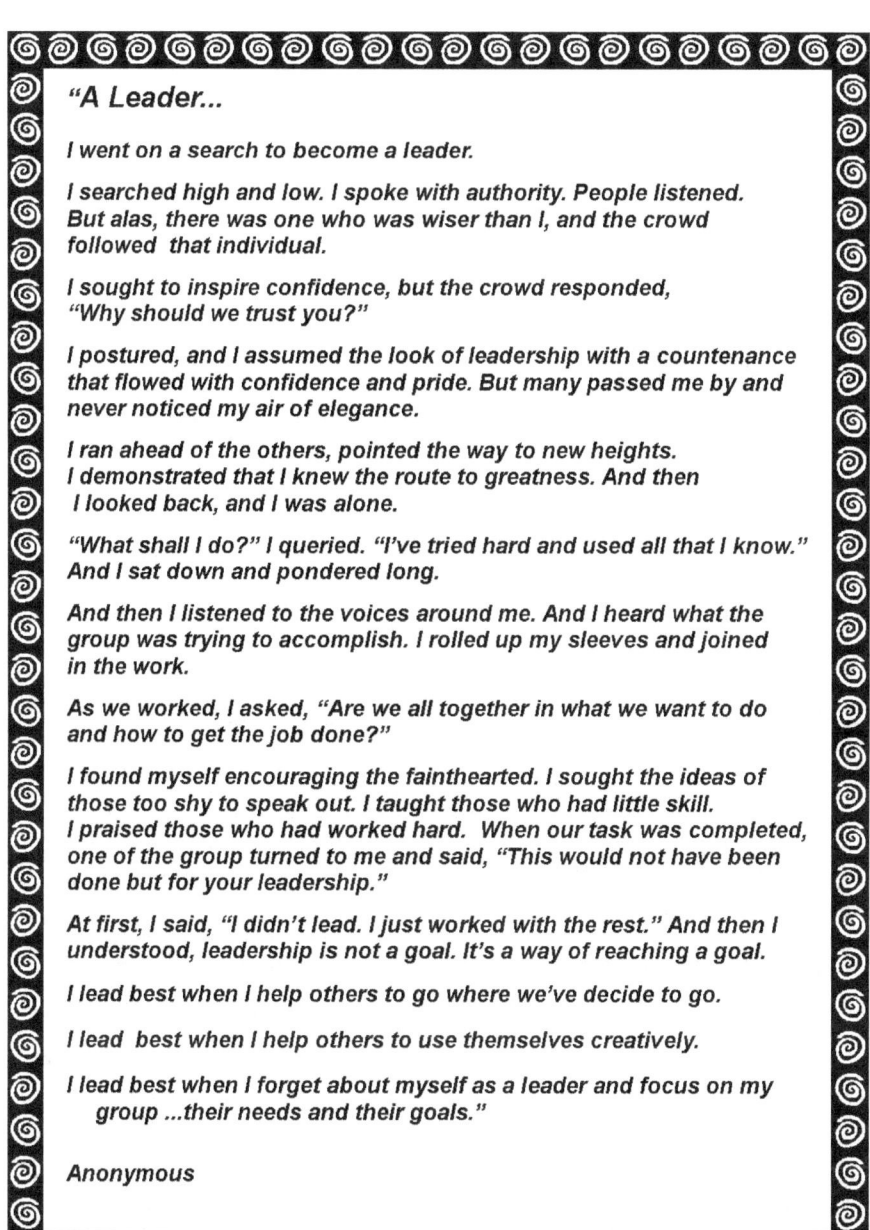

"A Leader...

I went on a search to become a leader.

I searched high and low. I spoke with authority. People listened. But alas, there was one who was wiser than I, and the crowd followed that individual.

I sought to inspire confidence, but the crowd responded, "Why should we trust you?"

I postured, and I assumed the look of leadership with a countenance that flowed with confidence and pride. But many passed me by and never noticed my air of elegance.

I ran ahead of the others, pointed the way to new heights. I demonstrated that I knew the route to greatness. And then I looked back, and I was alone.

"What shall I do?" I queried. "I've tried hard and used all that I know." And I sat down and pondered long.

And then I listened to the voices around me. And I heard what the group was trying to accomplish. I rolled up my sleeves and joined in the work.

As we worked, I asked, "Are we all together in what we want to do and how to get the job done?"

I found myself encouraging the fainthearted. I sought the ideas of those too shy to speak out. I taught those who had little skill. I praised those who had worked hard. When our task was completed, one of the group turned to me and said, "This would not have been done but for your leadership."

At first, I said, "I didn't lead. I just worked with the rest." And then I understood, leadership is not a goal. It's a way of reaching a goal.

I lead best when I help others to go where we've decide to go.

I lead best when I help others to use themselves creatively.

I lead best when I forget about myself as a leader and focus on my group ...their needs and their goals."

Anonymous

I love working with leaders. I figure, when I get them engaged, we can make some significant changes throughout the whole organization. I've written numerous books on the subject. Visit: **www.SuccessPublications.ca**

2008: Irene said yes….

As some who know me have realized, Irene and I have been spending a lot of time together over the past five years. We are now, as of October 4th, husband and wife. How cool is that!

We were on a repositioning cruise from Vancouver to Los Angeles and a few days in Las Vegas. Somewhere off the coast of Oregon, she said yes.

We were married by a local pastor in Las Vegas, at a little chapel just off the strip with our two friends **Robert and Christine Oxley** standing up for us. We flew home that evening and have been having fun blending our homes and lives as we move forward. Irene loves to travel, so I see lots of adventures in our futures. And, now I don't have to always travel alone.

Bob and Irene following their marriage ceremony in Las Vegas. October 4th, 2008

2009

2009: Passion + Pride = Performance

Interesting equation! Bet you are wondering what it means? Bet you figured out I will share that idea with you as you continue to read. Correct!

I think all of us, regardless of what role or roles we play in our lives, want to succeed. I have met very few people who *consciously* decide they want to live a life of failure or disappointment. Success is one of the words we use to rate our performance. So is failure. Both are subjective and all to often, used in comparison to the performance, or lack thereof, of someone else.

Life is challenge enough without setting ourselves up for grief as we observe someone else's life or performance and use it to criticize our own. During the recent 23rd Winter Olympics hosted by Canada in British Columbia, there were 14 Gold medals won by Canada. Now that is quite a feat (a record actually) and one we can own. There were also Golds, Silvers, and Bronze medals won by many athletes, including Canadians, from around the world. While I applaud the accomplishments of those athletes who earned medals (I must admit once in awhile I got patriotic when we did well), I wonder if we missed the point somehow?

In so many ways each of the athletes did well in representing their county by showing up ready to compete and giving 'their' best as they competed. Many finished their Olympic experience with a personal best. Too many went home thinking they had failed or at worst, wishing they had succeeded.

We do that in our personal and professional lives all too often. Miss a sale or a deadline. Make a mistake at work. Forget your spouse's special day. Every day we have opportunities to celebrate our performance, learn from experience, and to live our lives as an adventure.

Ok, so here is the rationale behind the above equation.

Passion: When we live our lives with passion, we bring something more to each day. When we live our lives with passion, we enhance what we bring to the table in our business dealings and how we treat our clients. When we live our lives with passion, we love those we care about just a bit more vividly and 'passionately' too.

I tap into and focus my passion when I am on stage to challenge my audiences to think, to act, to live, and to move outside their comfort zone. I am, myself, challenged to do likewise.

Pride: When we take pride in what we do, we stretch and create a higher standard in our work and our interaction with our colleagues, our clients, and our competitors. When we take pride in what we do, we put that little something extra into our ordinary day to day tasks and make every endeavour and activity count.

I take pride in being a professional and seek to deliver 'extra' value to each client, into each article, and into each product I produce.

Performance: When we tap into our passion and express pride in a job well done or a life well lived, we perform at our 'personal' best. Wouldn't that be a life worth living? Live every day with a goal of making it your 'personal best', so far. Wow!

Let me share this poem with you. You might even recognize it as it has been shared around the world. It was written by my long-time friend, mentor, and fellow speaker, **Bill Clennan.** Bill shared how it came to be with us years ago when he gave us a personal copy. I have mine mounted and framed in my office in our country home.

He was golfing in the US many years ago (ok, quite awhile back) and was asked if a couple of black gentlemen could join him. He said yes and enjoyed a wonderful round of golf. Bill loved to golf... that was one of his passions... he told me, "If I can golf and give a speech, it's my greatest day."

One of the golfers was former Olympic gold medalist, **Jesse Owens** who did so well in the 1936 Summer Berlin Olympics. He showed the world that Hitler was totally wrong about the passion, pride, and performance of people of color. Hitler left in a fit of anger when he won, again and again.

Jesse told Bill the most interesting thing about his performance was no one even remembers who came in second, or third.

Here is what Bill captured in thought following that *impactful* conversation. Please keep its message to mind when you are talking with your teams, your families, and especially your kids. It is about **Passion + Pride = Performance** and doing your **'Personal Best'** in life, not just about winning.

"The contest lasts for moments
Though the training's taken years.
It wasn't the winning alone that was worth the work and the tears.
The applause will be forgotten, the prize will be misplaced.
But the long hard hours of practice will never be a waste.
For in trying to win, you build a skill.
You learn that winning depends on will.
You never grow by how much you win
You'll only grow by how much you put in.
So any new challenge you've just begun.
Put forth your best and you've already won."

(sadly, Bill is no longer with us, but his inspiration lives on)

2009: *"I have issues, but no problems"* Nando Parrado

I recently returned from attending our National Speakers association annual convention in Scottsdale, Arizona. Pretty warm! Our coolest day was only 106 F with most days in the 110-120 F range. Whew! Even took a break or two to cruise on the Marriott's Lazy River with some fellow Canadians. Nice way to break the heat wave.

It was a great time to reconnect with colleagues and friends; a wonderful shared experience in refocusing our efforts in being better in what we do and what we share with our audience. Definitely, worth the trip. Lots of thought-provoking presentations, breakout sessions, and conversations enroute to events and sessions. Hmmmm. I love the people in this industry.

Here is a sheer contrast to the heat: For 72 sub-arctic freezing days and 72 even colder nights, **Nando Parrado** (Miracle in the Andes) and his remaining teammates struggled to live and to survive after a tragic plane crash in the Andes Mountains. It was an experience that would change them forever. Only 17 survived and Nando lost many teammates as well as his mother and sister. Seeing and hearing his challenging struggle to live puts our day to day 'issues' into perspective. I'd had a long challenging day enroute to Phoenix for the annual NSA convention with canceled flights, taking a side trip to Vancouver instead of a direct flight, taking 12 hours vs. the scheduled 3½. After hearing Nando on the second day of our convention, I realized I too had issues, but no 'real' problems.

One of the highlights of the convention: Opening night saw my friend **Vince Poscente** (former Olympic ski racer) take the stage and captivate them as well. The highlight of the evening, for me, was seeing his 11-year old daughter **Alex Poscente**, introduce him. She was amazing and she wrote the introduction piece herself. I told her, *"I'm glad I will be retired before you enter the business"*. We both laughed.

Following his presentation, Vince was bogged down with well wishers and his book table was un-manned. I invited Alex to come with me to sign books for her dad. She did, to her delight and that of each who purchased one. A very special young lady who got a real taste of what her dad does for a living. And she liked it!

It was fun observing her and her dad as she would autograph each book and then hand it to him for his... more so when so many told her *"You were great up there... and your dad was ok too."* with a smile. Later she told me, *"You know, I kind of liked it when they said that."* I told her, *"I know your dad did!"*

Just dropped off my application to renew my Canadian Passport as I know I will not be going anywhere for the next couple of weeks. The old one was getting full, only a couple of empty pages left. Smile... but it has been *well used* in the last year or two and hopefully the new one will see a lot of the world too.

Talking with the folks from the Professional Speakers group in the Netherlands about speaking at their convention next March and the folks in India said something about next year.

I am very blessed to be able to do what I am doing and to have so many wonderful people in my life to share it and who encourage and push me past my comfort zone. One of the riches of this business is the amazing people who enrich my life.

Meet our newest members of Team Hooey. Dusty and Jasmin.

We got them from the Rescue society a year or so after we lost Nala. Irene said she wanted another kitty! So, I said, let's get two so they can keep each other company.

They are amazing additions to our life.

2009: Her name was Nala and she allowed me to LOVE her

Nala started her life 13 years ago as an abandoned barn kitten who was rescued by Irene's son, Alex. Nala was originally named Simba, of the Lion King fame, until 'he' was discovered to be a female. She became a *fuzzy* welcome member of the Gaudet family and was loved by all. She lost a front leg in a freak accident but learned to live without it and lived well.

She entered my life when Irene and I started dating and she was not open to sharing with a man, any man. Initially she would hiss, scratch, or bite when I attempted to pet her. Normally, I find animals easy to connect with and so I was challenged. As I spent more time with Irene and Nala, I took deliberate steps to befriend and to spoil her. She wanted to trust me; I could see it. But it took time, *a lot of time* for her to come around.

She allowed me to love her, and I did. I found myself talking to her when she was sleeping on the couch and would see her little tail wag in response. Irene and I would laugh when she would approach her snack dish under the coffee table and then look at me, as if to tell me it was empty. I would get up and give her some snacks. I'd look over when I was sitting at my computer in the Mundare office and there she was keeping me company.

After Irene and I were married, I loved that she would come up on the couch and snuggle behind my knees... as she fell asleep, a small paw would reach out to gently rest on my leg. I loved her as I loved her mom... smile.

She passed away peacefully, on my lap on Sunday (November 22nd), while Irene and I talked with her and petted her, tears running down our cheeks. She had been sick in the last week or so and we found her lying on the floor, too weak to even get on the couch, when we returned from visiting our CAPS Calgary friends.

We will miss her, a lot. We'll 'even' miss Irene's frustration with her when she got underfoot. Or, when she would decide it was time for us to be awake and climb on us early each morning to let us know. I'll miss her stretched on the bed across my arm when Irene was up early and off to work. Amazing how these warm little balls of fur can worm their ways into our hearts, by allowing us to love them.

We often encounter those who, initially, resist us, our friendships, our service, or our attempts to build a relationship. Like Nala, they allow us to earn the right to love them or to serve them in our professional roles. I remember going through a similar exercise with Missy, one of my sister's dogs. I am now Uncle Bob and they love me to death whenever I visit her and her husband. (PS: I love it!) We can continue doing what we can to earn their trust, or we can quit and move on. The choice is ours, but, from experience, the extra work is so worth it!

Christmas is coming and this is a great time to express our love for those who have allowed us to love them. Whether Christmas is *just a nice story* or a time to celebrate the reason behind the season, it is a great time to reach out and express your love, affection, and appreciation for the important people in your life.

Perhaps the perfect Christmas gift we can give is to love and allow ourselves to be loved in return. Her name was Nala and she allowed me to LOVE her.

2009: Hassle

The following email message appeared in my in-box about every 7 days... it serves as a little reminder and helps me keep my focus.

"Hi, **This is a hassle to remind you to**: 'Focus on appreciating and expressing my gratitude for the people, business opportunities, affluence, opportunities to touch people's lives, travel the world sharing my ideas, and to have so many people appreciate and purchase my writing and wisdom. I am so blessed!' **So, get to it!"**

Now, I admit I don't always open it to read, but simply seeing it appear reminds me to be grateful for the blessings in my life. I have many!

I love what I do and get paid very well for doing it. People buy and read or listen to what I have to say... pretty cool stuff. I have a network of real friends, colleagues and readers, like you, who support and encourage me. I have two homes, Egremont (in the country) and Mundare (in town) to take care of and enjoy... twice the snow, yeah.

I have the opportunity to travel the world sharing my ideas. **I have an amazing woman by my side** who inspires me to keep moving outside of my comfort zone and is such an amazing partner in what I do to serve you and my audiences. I could go on, but you get the picture.

I was out for lunch with my 96-year old (Egremont) neighbor Steve, who can be a bit *crusty* at times. I love the time I spend with him. He has a bad back and struggles to walk, more so when the snow makes it even more of a challenge for him. He was complaining about all the stuff he **couldn't do,** *anymore.* (Boy, can I relate, as I did something to mine in India and it is still very sore.)

Ever find yourself doing that? Me too. I reminded him (and myself) that there was *still* a myriad of things he could do; and that, at 96, he was still inspiring me.

I thought, we could use a bit of a reminder of the blessings, the good stuff, and great people in our lives. We are working through a challenging economic time and it is easy to lose focus on the positive things and important people in our lives. **Just a nudge from me this month.**

All the best for February. **I choose to make it a fabulous month**, just as I choose to not participate in 'this' recession. What will you choose?

"Gratitude is the healthiest of all human emotions. The more you express gratitude for what you have, the more likely you will have even more to express gratitude for." Zig Ziglar

I am so grateful for everyone who reads our e-zine or articles and has taken time to write and let us know what it meant to you. Thanks so much!

2009: On getting older...

By Irene Gaudet

Thought I'd managed to get away with it, but no, too many people reminding me that it's my birthday. There's all that 'twaddle' that says, "Don't feel bad about growing older, it's a privilege denied to many." and, "Youth is wasted on the young." but frankly when you get up and the bones creak and various parts don't work quite as well as they once did - it just sucks! (PS: Irene's birthday is the end of January)

I could think of it like my husband Bob does – as my **"Personal New Year"** – and that's a kind of cool idea, but that requires a little thought re-wiring.

Frankly, re-wiring old structures has always seemed a bit of a risky proposition to me. Never know what sort of a mess you might run into when you expose the foundation!

But, to tell the truth though, **I can't think of any other age I'd rather be right now – cause then I'd have to give back all this hard-won knowledge and experience!**

Wouldn't want to be 16 – no way – too much going on, too many life decisions to make, too many hormones! Wouldn't want to be 21 – with all that worry – will I get a job, should I get married, should I have kids? And as much as I love my kids, wouldn't want to be any age with small kids or, heaven forbid, teenagers – because it was just way too tough, especially as a single mom. I wouldn't give back any of those times, but neither would I want to relive them!

So, I guess that leaves me here – and to tell the truth, it's a pretty good here. I have two wonderful children who mean the world to me. I have a wonderful husband who is also my best friend. I have wonderful, special friends, and my life and occasionally give me that **'kick in the butt'** when I need it! I still have both my parents who constantly remind me of who I am and what is important.

I have a husband who demonstrates his love and care for me and challenges me to move outside of my comfort zone. (Actually, he is sometimes just a challenge... lol) I have a new career that I love and a web-design business that excites me.

I guess that is what a personal new year is about – you take stock of your life, find the good, resolve to work on the 'not as good as I would like' and move forward.

Robert Browning has always said it best: *"Grow old along with me! The best is yet to be, the last of life, for which the first was made. Our times are in his hand who saith, 'A whole I planned, youth shows but half; Trust God: See all, nor be afraid!'"*

Note from Irene's husband: Very smart woman I married! And very well said.

I do take my birthday (April) as a Personal New Year as that makes so much more sense than January 1st. **A time to reflect:**

- on how well I lived up to my intentions during the previous year;
- on how well I accomplished my business, life, and career goals;
- on where I have grown and the lessons I've learned along the way;
- on the many friends, clients, and colleagues who have blessed me;
- on what I want to accomplish during the next year;
- on what updated intentions will create my focus;
- on how I can enhance my abilities and skills to better serve my clients and more profitably build my business;
- on how I can be a better friend and encourager to my friends, colleagues, and family;
- and, on how I can be a better friend, lover, encourager, and husband to my amazing wife.

"Grow old along with me! The best is yet to be..." is on an antiqued wall plaque, Charlene (one of Irene's closest friends from work) gave us for a wedding present. It hangs above Irene's work area just to the right of mine and catches my eye on many occasions... **enough said!**

Note: Bob has been speaking around the globe for over 25 years. He'd love to come to your part of the world. **bhooey@mcsnet.ca www.ideaman.net**

Bob in Paris (2019) **https://youtu.be/HRN0HyChtvg**

Bob's new demo video: https://youtu.be/-fAFD9mkUPo

2009: *"The entrepreneur always searches for change, responds to it, and exploits it as an opportunity."* **Peter Drucker,** *Best selling author*

Life is interesting as we have opportunities presented to us on an ongoing basis. Often, they come disguised as problems or challenges. In business, and especially sales our long-term growth, success, and profitability are *directly* related to our ability to recognize opportunities.

Opportunities to:
- provide innovative, mutually profitable solutions for our clients.
- pioneer new ideas, methods, techniques, and sometimes create new business ideas that open a new industry.
- adapt our processes or adopt new ideas which better equip us to separate ourselves from the herd and better serve our clients.

Let me share an example with you. I worked with a Canadian client in various capacities. We trained their senior executives, coached their founder in his many presentations, and helped write a defining book for their team. One February while having lunch with their CEO and his wife, we got talking about helping their sales teams across Canada. In our discussions we brainstormed an idea for a simple and systematic way to keep them focused, provide sales training, and discuss new ideas. We even came up with a name. I looked at my client and said, *"It sounds like, if I build it, you'll buy it."* and he said, *"YES!"*. We discussed a fee to develop it (very reasonable) and I said, *"We'll have it for you by the beginning of March."* And, **Secret Selling Tips** was launched to become its own business unit for us; a very profitable business unit with clients across North America and around the globe.

This opportunity presented itself in a simple conversation. Had I not responded from a perspective of, 'How can I serve you?' I would have missed it.

- How many opportunities do you miss because you don't take the time to ask questions or investigate the challenges?
- How many do you miss due to fear or being timid and not being willing to stretch past your comfort zone into the winner's zone?
- How many do you miss because you are afraid to ask or risk rejection?

Let me share another example. As some of you know I had the pleasure of being invited to speak in Vladivostok, Eastern Russia last June. This is how that came about. I was speaking at a leadership event the previous September and noticed that they had people attending from Russia as well as across North America. I actually stopped during my presentation and asked, "I understand we

104

have some folks here from Russia. Where are you?" A couple of hands went up, so I asked, **"Can I talk to you when I am done? I would love to come and speak in your country."** I continued my presentation and met with them later.

They returned home and a month or so later, I got an email which started the conversation for my trip. Fabulous people and place to visit. I have found life is an adventure when you see and seize the opportunities that come your way.

2009: Ships at anchor seem peaceful...

They were not designed to *just* sit... They were *designed* to sail forth from a safe harbor, to tackle unforgiving seas and uncertain winds in search of other ports.

Point to Ponder – We, too, were *designed* to risk and sail forth...

"The brave may not live forever – but the cautious do not live at all!"
Sir Richard Branson

- When was the last time you took a *calculated* risk?
- When was the last time you pushed yourself outside of your comfort zone?
- When was the last time you set some seemingly outrageous goals and dared to tell the world about them?

As mentioned in our Christmas note, ***"This is a great time to push ahead when your competition is running for safety,"*** but it takes courage to risk and to push yourself into the winner's zone.

Just digging into an interesting book by **Sam Geist**. **"Execute... or Be Executed."** My friend **Kim Yost** recommended it. Author, Geist asks, *"Why is Wal-Mart so dominant? Why is Southwest Airlines so popular? Why is McDonald's doing so well?"* His answer, *"They execute! The winners always out-execute the laggards."*

They, like the companies **Jim Collins** interviewed for **Good to Great**, *'executed their strategies'* which helped them evolve into exceptional companies.

So, here we are at the launch of another New Year. A new year with a blank canvas that can be painted or created in any image you envision. A year in which you can chart a new course, make corrections on a current one, and sail confidently to greater successes and adventures.

- What are you going to risk this year?
- What are you committed to doing that will astound those around you should you succeed?
- Have you started it yet?

Irene and I were doing some Christmas shopping and running errands in Edmonton a while back. We stopped into Vo's to get her nails filled and *decorated* for Christmas. I wandered around window shopping and then came back to sit and wait for her to finish. While I was sitting, waiting, I observed an interesting conversation between a 20 *something* young woman and an 80 *something* senior who were sitting side by side having their nails done.

What caught my attention was the older lady chattering away gayly and the amazing animation in her face as she did so. I also noticed the younger woman was carefully listening and commenting back. They were having a conversation, not just being polite. This went on for a good fifteen minutes or more with the younger woman good humouredly sharing back with her. From snippets I overheard, it seemed the older lady was on her own with no real family around. That can be tough at this time of year.

As the older lady left, she did so with a genuine smile on her face, an energy much younger than her years and a, **"I hope I see you again"** to the younger one, who replied, "I'm in here from time to time and I hope to see you too."

2009: *"Dream as though you will live forever, live as though you'll die today."* James Dean

Perhaps you've heard of the recent deaths of veteran entertainers Ed McMahn, Farah Fawcett, Billy May, and Michael Jackson? Unless you were trekking out of electronic touch, of course you have... their passing has been **all over** the media of late.

While I am saddened to hear of their deaths, I find it a bit strange to see the media hype and the hysteria that follows the death of a celebrity. Are their deaths of so much more importance that the death of a loved one or a close friend? **NO! just more newsworthy... and therein lies the real sadness.**

I understand their passing creates pain in the lives of their immediate families and close friends... but, frankly in light of other, more impactful news items I am a bit at a loss to all the hype.

With people in Iran being beaten and killed for simply standing up for their rights and in search of democracy... media attention on the death of celebrities seems somewhat misplaced and inappropriate to me.

Don't get me wrong... I've appreciated their talent and the entertainment value each provided by their skills over the years. I just think there are more important things we should think about.

Some of those things are closer to home:

- Telling those we hold close that we love and appreciate them for the 'gifts' they are in our lives.
- Letting our clients know we are 'still' here to serve them and appreciate their support and trust during this time of turmoil.
- Investing in our personal and professional development by adding to and honing our skills.
- Celebrating life and enjoying the laughter and love of our families and friends.
- Leveraging our outreach by working with colleagues to enhance what we offer our clients.
- Being involved in our communities and in the lives of those around us by 'investing' our time, our skills, and at times our finances.
- Investing time challenging our brains by reading, listening to recordings by experts who can help us move out of our comfort zones.

I sincerely hope when my time comes that a few might mourn my passing. Frankly, I am more focused on what impact my life makes while I live it than my death. **It is our life and what we do with it that really matters.**

Life is at 'best' a short time on this earth. Each day is an adventure to be lived and loved. Treat each day as the *'present'* it is and give of yourself.

2009: You always get paid... sometimes it is cash - sometimes it is cookies

Had an interesting and challenging presentation last month... I was invited to keynote the Lamont High 2009 Graduation on June 12th.

Very interesting evening and presentation. Had the 36 capped and gowned grads sitting on a *very hot* raised stage behind me with their parents, families, and school staff in the more traditional location out front. Definitely a *work-out* swiveling to speak to both groups as I sought the words to share respectively.

Part of my payment was a box of homemade chocolate chip cookies baked by **Meghan Guglich** who was the class valedictorian.

The *real* payment was in being able to share a few ideas I trust will be of benefit when they leave their protected High School environment and travel into the real world of work and additional education.

I shared with them that now was the perfect time for them to be entering the real world, as we needed their fresh ideas and enthusiasm. One of the local politicians had *'cliché-ed'* them with... **You are our future!** I told them I wasn't going to say 'that' as I felt that put unfair pressure on them.

We are, each of us, responsible for our own future and what we invest today impacts our tomorrows. I told them I planned on being around for awhile and was busy working on my own future.

2009: Are you happy?

Some wise person once said, **"Most people are as happy as they make up their minds to be!"** Not sure who said it, but it makes sense to me.

I celebrated my 60th birthday, twice. Spent a week with Irene at a resort outside of Holguin, Cuba relaxing, reflecting, and enjoying the sun and fun. We had a wonderful time and were very well treated by the resort staff as well as the folks in a small town close by. I was impressed at how *genuinely* happy these folks were, in-spite of their not having a standard of living any of us would envy. They smiled, they laughed, and they shared their joy with those around them. I loved it. Not like the complaining too often seen in our northern neighborhoods.

On the bus enroute to the airport for our return trip, our guide told us stories of what had been happening in Cuba. He told us they had recently shut down half of their sugar factories as the machinery wasn't working well enough to justify the expense of production.

He told us about the dark time in their history when the Soviet empire imploded and pulled out of Cuba. Over-night their country's income dropped by 72%.

How would you react if you lost nearly 3/4 of your income in one blow? How would you live? I can relate, as I went through something like that following 9-11. That was a dark time in my business and yet, looking back, it forced me to evaluate my business and make some foundational changes that have helped in our success over the past 5 or 6 years. Often, in hindsight, challenges can be our greatest teachers.

Overnight there was literally no money for workers. People were sent home to wait until the Government came up with a solution and what little income was radically reduced. Our guide told us it was a tough time and many people got angry... angry at the Soviets, angry at the Government, angry at... well, you get the idea.

Then he said something very insightful:
 "Many of us decided we could either be out of work and angry... or be out of work and play domino's ..." followed by a big smile and a laugh which was shared by most of us on the bus.

His insightful comments shared a glimpse into the spirits of so many of the Cuban people who philosophically adjusted to the challenges and realities and decided to make the best of it.

Following that challenge, the Cubans began looking at tourism as a viable source of revenue and employment. In fact, in order to work at the resorts and in the tourism industry, Cubans go to school for extensive training.

One of the crew on a 'cat' cruise we took mid week told us he had lost his 'complete' house and everything in it during the recent hurricane. He was working to rebuild while his wife and baby son lived at her mothers. He told me he figured it would take about two years to earn enough to buy the basic materials to reconstruct a very *basic* shelter for his family. His home was destroyed and, yet, you'd never know it by his demeanor and genuine smile.

I found myself listening to the 'minor' complaints of my fellow Canadians as we flew home and in the airport in Toronto and later, Edmonton. Guess they didn't see what I saw or perhaps they were just 'tourists' and along for the ride.

I celebrated my birthday, again, on May 15th when my amazing friends at The Brick decided to host a birthday lunch for myself and Irene. I am so blessed to have such wonderful friends and colleagues in my life.

I love working with them and I love spending time with them. In-spite very demanding, hectic work schedules and being impacted by some of the same harsh economic challenges we all face, they still make time to have fun to be happy, and to encourage others. That is one of the reasons they are a 'great' company and I am confident they will weather this storm and come out even stronger. As **Warren Buffet** teaches, invest in the people who create value for the company.

Many people quizzically comment on my age... many can't believe I am 'actually' 60 years old. They think I am quite a bit younger... But, as I tell them, *"Think about it? Would I lie about being this age?"* I was thinking about that and other than good genes I think one of the reasons I don't look my age is my attitude towards life.

Overall, I am a pretty happy guy and for the most part a pretty positive, pro-active one as well. I love what I do, I find a sense of satisfaction in tackling challenges, and in giving encouragement and innovative ideas to others. That undoubtedly has an impact on how I look. I bet my big smile makes my face look younger too... These wrinkles are love and laugh lines and I cherish each one. An old Irish blessing... I wanted to share its wisdom with you.

May you have Happiness

May your joys be as bright as the morning and your shadows merely shadows that fade in the sunlight of love.
May you have enough happiness to keep you sweet
Enough trials to keep you strong
Enough sorrow to keep you human
Enough failure to keep you humble
Enough success to keep you eager
Enough friends to give you comfort
Enough faith and courage in yourself to banish sadness
Enough wealth to meet your needs

And one thing more: **Enough determination to make each day a more wonderful day that the one before.**

2009: *"Dream lofty dreams, and as you dream, so shall you become. Your vision is the promise of what you shall one day be; your ideal is the prophecy of what you shall at last unveil."* **James Allen**

What do you dream about? What thoughts flow through your mind when you find yourself drawn away from the normalcy of life or the routine in your role or career? How does that dream line up with who you are becoming now? How does it line up with who and what you want to present to the world as your testament or life statement?

I remember sitting in a small fish and chips place in Adelaide, NSW with my new friend **Peter J. Daniels** about 15 or so years ago. I had just told him of my dream of being a professional speaker and what that meant to me. He smiled kindly and challenged me to explode my dreams to *"dream big dreams"*. He went on to explain that small dreams had very little power to push me through the tough times of challenge that would surely come as the rain in the spring. He was right.

So, I pass on that challenge to each of my readers. What is your dream? Is it big enough to power you through the times of challenge? We are entering the halfway point in our year, how are you doing? Have you found, as I have, that some areas have far surpassed even your greatest dreams or perhaps a few areas have fallen way short? Push on my friend, dig into the power of your dreams, and refocus your energy to make the second half of this year your greatest yet. The best song has yet to be written, the greatest sale is yet to be signed, the best team is yet to be formed, your best family times are yet to be shared, and your greatest achievement is still within you, waiting to emerge.

As my friend, **Kim Duke** (Sales Divas) reminds me... work at least 3 to 6 months out to make sure I am as productive and busy as I desire. I hear you Kim. Have a wonderful June and send this ezine along to someone who you feel will benefit from reading it.

2009: Use your imagination

"The great successful men and women of the world have used their imagination...they think ahead and create their mental picture in all its details, filling in here, adding a little there, altering this a bit and that a bit, but steadily building – steadily building." **Robert Collier**

This quote provides a snapshot of my life, successes, and learning experiences. I have been fortunate to be given a good imagination and, by use and discipline, enhance it to the point where I can visualize and create projects mentally that take months to create and process in real time.

Our **Foundational Success: Building Blocks for Personal and Professional Success** is a case in point. I was asked to sit on the CAPS Foundation as a Trustee at our last CAPS convention in Toronto. I came up with the idea and registered the domain name that weekend. Then I got approval from our Foundation Board to go ahead and create the project. I approached many guest experts and authors (29 of them said yes) and we began working on it "... filling in here, adding a little there, altering this a bit and that a bit, but steadily building – steadily building". We hope you will check it out and invest in your future by buying your own copy.

Visit: **www.SuccessPublications.ca**

This quote also applies to what we have done with our **Ideas @ Work!** Ezine since we launched it in April 4 years ago. We made changes and improvements, changed delivery systems, purged our lists to ensure those who really wanted it were subscribed, and slowly added a personal element that so many of you have commented you like. Thanks for being with us on our journey.

This applies to my business as well. Over the past dozen or so years we have been building and learning and editing and adapting. In each case with a focus of improving what we do, enhancing what we bring to the table, and how we can better serve our audiences and readers.

Along the way, a few books and other products and services like **Secret Selling Tips** have been created and each 'new' adventure has taught us 'new' skills.

My life, too, is no exception to the building process. There have been a lot of learning experiences, some very nice successes, and a few accolades and recognition along the way. There have been some serious challenges that caused me to re-think, refocus, and re-energize what I was doing. But, looking back...in each case we built on what we learned.

My life became more fulfilled when Irene and I reconnected; and as our relationship and friendship grew, so did I. I am extremely blessed to have her as an active partner in life and in helping me serve you. I celebrated **My Personal New Year** in Cuba and took some time to reflect on the past 60 years.

I took some time to dream about the next 30 or so. I'll tell you more about it in subsequent issues. Thanks for your support over this past year. I trust we have been able to bring some additional value into your lives, your careers, and your organizations.

2009: Point to Ponder - "The greatest attitude is gratitude!"

What are you grateful for? I saw this reader-board next to a local church the other day while driving in Edmonton. Got me thinking about what I was grateful for; more so since we celebrated Canadian Thanksgiving last month and our American friends celebrate theirs later this month.

You've probably heard it said, **"Your attitude determines your altitude!"** I believe that to be true and constantly encourage my readers and audiences to push themselves **out of their comfort zone into their winner's zone**. I recently told a group of College level interior design students that their professionalism starts with an attitude and that 'their' professionalism was one of the attitudes that would give them a competitive edge in life and business.

I told them about attending a kitchen design specialist course in Boston back in the 70's where I first heard, **"Professionalism starts with an Attitude!"** from my soon to be long-time friend, **Robert Oxley**, CKD. I learned from my own experience that "Professionalism" may start with an attitude, but it is proven by our actions. I believe our **'attitude of gratitude'** can differentiate us from our competition, endear us to our clients and colleagues, and help us build long-term, mutually supportive and productive relationships. Being grateful for their patronage is part of my passion.

So, what are you grateful for?

I am grateful for all of these and more:
- That God loves me and does so, even when I mess up.
- That my wife Irene does too, smile!
- That I have a wonderful woman to share my life as my wife, partner, best friend, lover, snuggler, proof-reader, confidant, executive assistant, travel buddy, encourager, challenger, and so much more... I am truly blessed!

- That my clients, around the world, entrust me with their teams and give me the privilege of sharing my ideas and encouraging them to stretch and to grow.
- That I have a career that challenges me to grow and to push myself; one which I love and that my passion has become a bridge to creating my dreams.
- That my writing has found readers around the world who appreciate and apply the innovative ideas I share from my observations and experience.
- That I am able to continually learn and leverage that learning in what I do in my life and my career.
- That I am able to travel the globe both on a personal basis and professionally. And that Irene is able to be with me on many of these adventures.
- In addition, that I have so many wonderful people – friends, colleagues, and family members in my life. People who love me, encourage me, push me to grow; and to actively move out of my comfort zone.

So, what are you grateful for?

2009: I dare you!

Remember growing up and being dared to do something? Remember how often you **actually** accomplished it, in spite of your own self doubts and fears? Well, I want to share a big DARE with you. But first, let me tell you the quick story of a young man named Bill, who responded to a personal DARE and changed his world and perhaps ours as well.

Bill was not a healthy boy; you might even have called him 'sickly'. His family moved from the country to the city where he encountered a teacher who was serious about health. As he wrote later, *"It was like he had singled me out."* His teacher, George Krall challenged him one day. He looked straight at Bill and said, *"I dare you to be the healthiest boy in class!"*

Young Bill responded and soon built a body that equaled and outlasted the strongest boys in his class. In fact, he never lost a day at work because of illness and lived a healthy and productive life. He served honorably during the 1st World War and returned to lead his fledgling company to greater success and profit during the great depression. He passed away in 1955, at 85, when the average life expectancy was a good 20 years lower, in part because he responded to that dare.

Bill launched a company which grew to be one of North America's largest corporations, providing employment for thousands of people. People who were challenged or dared by their president and later Chairman of the Board to push themselves to be strong, to be creative, to take risks, to build character, and to share with others. For nearly 40 years, Bill wrote a weekly inspirational *"Monday Morning Message"* for his employees, colleagues, and associates.

In a 1955 Monday Morning Message, when he was 84, he pointed out the personal significance of some of these unchanging fundamentals. *"Some folks are continually making changes,"* he said. *"I flatter myself that I like new ventures and new experiences. But when it comes to fundamentals, I believe in finding the right foundations and building on them. I'm a poor changer.* **For instance, here are some of the fundamentals I have never changed:** *I have been a church member for over 60 years; married to one wife for over 60 years; a lodge member for over 60 years; and a Purina man for over 60 years."*

Young Bill in this story is, of course, **William H. Danforth**, founder of the Ralston Purina Company, founder of the American Youth Foundation Camps, and author of 14 books including, **"I Dare You!"**

The copy I bought in 1976 was in its 26th printing. Bill Danforth's life and his writings have challenged hundreds of thousands (*including me*) to live life as an adventure and to stretch and grow in our careers and in our service to others.

I want to leave you with the following personal challenge:

I Dare You:

To believe in yourself, your experience, and your skills.
To push yourself to learn and hone your skills for greater success.
To take at least one course or field of study every quarter to enhance your skills.
To take increased responsibility and personal leadership in your role.
To tap into your creativity and allow innovation to flow.
To support and encourage your fellow team members to grow.
To never allow anyone or anything to stop you from succeeding in your role and in life.

I dare you to be the example for others in living life as an adventure and pushing past your comfort zone into the winner's zone.

I can offer this guarantee... if you do these things you will be ready, stronger and better positioned to succeed when 'this' recession is over. You will emerge a leader who has proven their worth.

2009: *"Life is what we make it, always has been, always will be."* Grandma Moses

Did you know that Sept 7th was Grandma Moses Day? **Grandma Moses**, born in 1860, first picked up her brush when she was 78. She created more than 1,600 original works of art before she put down her brush and died at the age of 101.

Moses was one of the most successful and famous artists in America and possibly the best-known American artist in Europe. Featured on radio, television, and in mass-market publications, she was arguably the first artist to become a media superstar. Grandma Moses invented a unique style that proved enormously popular, and its influence may be seen in art and illustration to this day.

You know, today is a great day to start something new or to renew: a new career, a comeback, a new success, a hobby, a sport, a relationship or... whatever you desire and dreamed of doing. Why not start now!

Life is short at best! We may not all live to be 101, but we can choose to live each day that we are given. Each is a gift, which is why they are called the 'present'.

When I was growing up, we used to go on driving vacations and primarily we visited 'relatives.' I have to admit, I didn't always enjoy them, which might be part of my motivation for more exotic or beach-based trips as I got older. Mom and Dad used to look forward to them and I wondered why? Now that I am older and perhaps a bit wiser, I am beginning to understand. It is about nurturing the relationships with the people in our lives.

Irene and I just returned home from a 10-day road vacation. Along the way we made the time to visit with friends and family and to renew relationships. Each moment we shared with our friends and family added to our trip and to our lives.

- Each one inspired me in not so obvious ways. My CAPS friend **Hugh Culver** is looking for ways to enhance his business and his ability to attract new clients. Our coffee and conversation sparked my mind with some new ways to try.
- Irene's **aunt Eva** (a die-hard Canucks fan) showered us with her gracious hospitality and love and we were made better for our time together.
- My cousin **Ann** just came back from a trip to Costa Rica with her two half sisters. She was able to find them and has built new relationships with them in the past couple of years.

116

- My cousins **Betty and Pete** (from Sidney) shared part of their day with us. Betty is in her early 80's and Peter is nearly 90 and, yet, they still have fun together. I have a 30-year contract with Irene that comes up when I am 89. (SMILE)
- My long time NSA friend and encourager **Bonnie Dean** and her husband David have had a very challenging year (health and family) but you'd never know it from their positive outlook and confident manner. Worth the trip down to Bellingham for a visit. Irene is going to help her with her websites and that is cool.

Each inspired me to push ahead, to try new things, and to follow the passion that stirs my soul. Each reminded me how precious each day is and that I have someone special to share it with now. Each is living their life by their own set of guidelines and handling the challenges it gives them with dignity and delight. I am privileged to have been able to spend brief moments with them.

I love the career I am learning and living, even with its challenges. I love the involvement with the people it has brought into my life which have made me better and made my life richer. My clients, my colleagues, my audiences and readers, and of course my extended family. Each of you have enriched my life and I thank you.

My challenge for you this month: As the kids return to school... what new thing will you undertake to learn in the next while?

2009: *"Be glad of life because it gives you the chance to love and to work and to play and to look up at the stars."* Henry van Dyke

As I write this **Point to Ponder,** I look out my office window to a dreary, wet day, again. Three times yesterday I was interrupted by rain showers and even hail as I attempted to start another project on the lower 'mojito' deck. Interesting how something like rain can dampen your spirits, if you let it. And, at other times, like a hot day, a gentle rain can be so welcome.

Rain is a natural part of life and is necessary on so many levels. The new trees, shrubs, and plants we just put in need it to establish themselves, to drive their roots deep into the soil, and to live. They need rain so they can grow and bring forth flowers and fruit for all to enjoy. We've been doing lots of work on the outside of our place in the country with new decks, pergolas, built-in seating, and new flower and garden beds.

Although it has been a labor of love it has been physically demanding for a 'Bob' who is *slightly* more mature than 20 years ago, or even 5 years ago. My body tells me daily that I have used it to the max and at times perhaps a bit more.

I've been making observations about gardening and building that very much relate to how we conduct our lives and build our businesses. Irene and I have been working as a team on many of these projects to make this retirement place one we will both enjoy for years to follow. I'll share more about that in upcoming note. I'll bet some of these lessons from nature will show up as stories in future presentations around the world.

I do know that how we do one thing is often how we do everything.

I know we can learn and profit from our lessons. I remember saying (quite often) **"Failure can become fuel for growth (fertilizer) when we don't rush to move on and take the time to sift through the lesson for the gems and growth stones, we need to make a new path".**

Speaking of stones, I found out I have a rock garden; no, really a rock garden. I bet I've dug up nearly 2000 pounds (maybe more) of rocks from the one garden plot we are making so there would be room for the blueberries, strawberries, saskatoons, and high bush cranberries, as well as room for a vegetable garden.

One rock was well above 300 pounds and we had a neighbor come over with his tractor and front-end loader to move it. But despite the rocks in the path, I can hardly wait until we get a taste of the fruits of our labor.

In life, and in business there are times when you have to dig up the rocks that prevent you from planting and growing. At times you need to repeatedly work the soil before you can plant your latest ideas. And then, you need to water it, fertilize it and make sure the weeds don't choke it out. Gardening can be hard work.

So is building a successful career or business. What you put into it is often returned multiplied.

A few years ago, I transplanted a few raspberry canes when I moved out here and waited to see if they would catch. They did and each year they have expanded (by themselves) and each year we are able to pick larger amounts to enjoy. Our lives and our businesses take a similar growth path.

Work your plot, plant good ideas, water and nurture them until you get to reap the rewards. Enjoy. May this fall be a time of harvest and success!

2009: Surprise!

Awoke one morning to Irene saying, "There's a tree down in the back yard!" And it was....one of the branches from our majestic 55-year old maple had snapped and fallen during the night. Not a storm that we heard, although there was a lot of rain. It wasn't rotten – just got tired of carrying the weight, I guess.

I went out and started clearing back the smaller branches. Amazingly it had missed the house. I could have hit the van normally parked there but since it was fully loaded for a trip to goodwill it was parked further up on the driveway. So, no property damage... just lots of work.

My neighbor Paul was home and brought over his JLG (man lift and front-end loader). We went way up and started trimming back the branches so we could get to the break. Along the way we cleared off all the other branches that extended near the house. It was a long day cutting and clearing, but, in the end, we were able to get it all out. We'll have a great big bonfire at his place after the first snow.

Irene couldn't watch as we cut away. She said it was like losing a member of the family. This tree provided shade in the yard and on the back deck. It also provided shelter for multitudes of birds on our property. We now need to use the blinds over the kitchen sink as the sun shines in – sometimes too brightly!

Made me think! Often, we carry loads that are too much for us. When we are resilient, we can get away with it, but eventually they will overwhelm us, and something might snap. Take a moment to rethink what you are carrying and see if you can let some of it go... we want you around for a long time.

About the author

Bob 'Idea Man' Hooey is a charismatic, confident leader, corporate trainer, inspiring facilitator, Emcee, prolific author, and award-winning motivational keynote speaker on leadership, creativity, success, business innovation, and enhancing team performance.

Using personal stories drawn from rich experience, he challenges his audiences to engage his **Ideas At Work!** – To act on what they hear, with clear, innovative building-blocks and field-proven success techniques to increase their effectiveness. Bob challenges them to hone specific 'success skills' critical to their personal and professional advancement.

Bob outlines real-life, results-based, innovative ideas personally drawn from 29 plus years of rich leadership experience in retail, construction, small business, entrepreneurship, manufacturing, association, consulting, community service, and commercial management.

Bob's conversational, often humorous, professional, and sometimes-provocative style continues to inspire and challenge his audiences across North America. Bob's motivational, innovative, challenging, and practical **Ideas At Work!** have been successfully applied by thousands of leaders and professionals across the globe. Busy man – productive man!

Bob is a frequent contributor to North American consumer, corporate, association, trade, and on-line publications on leadership, success, employee motivation and training; as well as creativity and innovative problem solving, priority and time management, and effective customer service. He is the inspirational author of 30 plus publications, including several best-selling, print, e-books, reader style e-pubs, and a Pocket Wisdom series.

Visit: **www.SuccessPublications.ca** for more information.

Retired, award winning kitchen designer, Bob Hooey, CKD-Emeritus was one of only 75 Canadian designers to earn this prestigious certification by the US based National Kitchen and Bath Association.

In December 2000, Bob was given a special CAPS National Presidential award **"…for his energetic contribution to the advancement of CAPS and his living example of the power of one"** in addition to being elected to the CAPS National Board. He has been recognized by the National Speakers Association and other groups for his leadership contributions.

Bob is a co-founder and a Past President of the CAPS Vancouver Chapter and served as 2012 President of the CAPS Edmonton Chapter. He is a member of the NSA-Arizona Chapter, a charter member of the Canadian Association of Professional Speakers as well as the Global Speakers Federation. He has retired (December 2013) as a Trustee from the CAPS Foundation. In 2019, Bob became a charter member of PSA Spain and will be returning to speak April 2020.

In 1998, Toastmasters International recognized Bob **"…for his professionalism and outstanding achievements in public speaking"**. That August in Palm Desert, California Bob became the 48th speaker in the world to be awarded this prestigious professional level honor as an **Accredited Speaker**. He has been inducted into their Hall of Fame on numerous occasions for his leadership contributions.

Bob has been honoured by the United Nations Association of BC (1993) and received the **CANADA 125 award** (1992) for his ongoing leadership contributions to the community. In 1998, Bob joined 3 other men to sail a 65-foot gaff rigged schooner from Honolulu, Hawaii to Kobe, Japan, barely surviving a 'baby' typhoon enroute.

In November 2011 Bob was awarded the Spirit of CAPS at their annual convention, becoming the 11th speaker to earn this prestigious CAPS National award. Visit: **www.ideaman.net/SoC.htm**

Bob loves to travel and his speaking and writing have allowed him to visit 46 countries so far. Perhaps your organization would like to bring Bob in to share a few ideas with your leaders and teams around the globe.

Visit: **www.HaveMouthWillTravel.com** for more information. Drop him a line at bhooey@mcsnet.ca

Copyright and license notes

Success Publications, a division of Creativity Corner Inc.
Box 10, Egremont, Alberta T0A 0Z0
www.successpublications.ca
Creative office: 1-780-736-0009

I raise a glass to each of you as you work your way through this collection of writings and ponderings. Over the years I have encountered some amazing people who have added zest, smiles, tears, and love in my life.

To each of you, I say thanks! You have enriched my life and this little book is my gift, in part, as a way to say thanks for everything you've done for me as I journeyed around the globe. It can be a challenge being a speaker, trainer and author at times. It is so much more fun when we have amazing people, like you, to share it with…

Acknowledgements, credits

As with each of my books, a very special dedication of this piece of myself, to the two people who meant the most to me, my folks **Ron and Marge Hooey**. Sadly, both my parents left this earthly realm in 1999. I still miss our time together and your encouragement and love. I was blessed with the two of you in my life.

To my inspiring wife and professional proof-reader and publications coach, **Irene Gaudet**, who loves, encourages, and supports me in my quest to continue sharing my **Ideas At Work!** across the world.

Thank you seems so inadequate for your timely work in helping make my writing and my client service better! I love the time we spend together!

My thanks to the many people who have encouraged me in my growth as a leader, speaker, and engaging trainer in each area of expertise.

To my colleagues and friends in the National Speakers Association **(NSA)**, the Canadian Association of Professional Speakers **(CAPS)**, and the Global Speakers Federation **(GSF)** who continually challenge me to strive for success and increased excellence.

To my many **Toastmasters** friends and family around the world, to whom I owe an un-payable debt of gratitude for your investment, encouragement, time, and support when I was just starting down this path; and oh, so rough around the edges.

To my great audiences, fellow leaders, students, coaching clients, and readers across the globe who share their experiences and enjoyment of my work. Your positive and supportive feedback encourages me to keep working on additional programs and success publications like this updated version. My experience with you creates the foundation for additional real-life experiences I can take from the stage to the page, the classroom to the boardroom.

My thanks to a *select* few friends for your ongoing support and 'constructive' abuse. You know who you are. ☺

Disclaimer

When I am home between adventures and business trips, you'll often see me sitting with my two furry kids.

Each of them added love, enjoyment and of course a bit of work in our lives. But we love them to pieces. In life we have a mixture of joy and sorrow… choose to embrace joy and let your life be a beacon to others.

What they say about Bob 'Idea Man' Hooey

As I travel across North America and around the globe, sharing my **Ideas At Work!,** I am fortunate to get feedback and comments from my audiences and colleagues. These comments come from people who have been touched, challenged, or simply enjoyed themselves in one of my sessions or one of our publications.

I'd love to come and share some ideas with your organization.

"I've known Bob for several years and follow his activities in business with interest. I originally met Bob when he spoke for a Rotary Leadership Institute and got to know him better when he came to Vladivostok, Russia to speak to our leadership. **When you spoke, I thought you were one of us because you talked about our challenges just like yours.** *You could understand the others, which makes you a great speaker!"*
Andrey Konyushok, *Rotary International District 2225 Governor 2012-2013, far eastern Russia*

"I still get comments from people about your presentation. **Only a few speakers have left an impression that lasts that long.** *You hit a spot with the tourism people."* **Janet Bell,** *Yukon Economic Forums*

"We greatly appreciate **the energy and effort you put into researching and adapting your keynote to make it more meaningful to our member councils.** *Early feedback from our delegates indicates that this year's convention was one of our most successful events yet, and we thank you for your contribution to this success."* **Larry Goodhope,** *Executive Director Alberta Association of Municipal Districts and Counties*

"Thank you Bob; it is **always a pleasure to see a true professional at work.** *You have made the name 'Speaker' stand out as a truism - someone who encourages people to examine their lives and make adjustments. The personal stories you shared with your audience made such a great impression on everyone.* **The comments indicated you hit people right where it is important - in their hearts.** *Each of those in your audience took away a new feeling of personal success and encouragement."* **Sherry Knight,** *Dimension Eleven Human Resources and Communications*

"Bob is one of those rare individuals who knows how to tackle obstacles in life to reach his dreams. He takes each as a learning **experience and stretches for more.** *His compassion and genuine interest in others, make him an exceptional coach."* **Cindy Kindret,** *Training Manager, Silk FM Radio*

*"Without doubt, **I have gained immeasurable self-assurance.** Bob, your patience and your encouragement has been much appreciated. **I strongly recommend your course to anyone looking for self-improvement and professional development.**"* **Jeannie Mura**, *Human Resources Chevron Canada*

*"I am pleased to recommend Bob 'Idea Man' Hooey to any organization looking for a charismatic, confident speaker and seminar leader. I have seen Bob in action on several occasions, and he is ALWAYS on! Bob has the ability to grab his audience's attention and keep it. Quite simply, **if Bob is involved - your program or seminar is guaranteed to succeed.**"* **Maurice Laving**, *Coordinator Training and Development, London Drugs*

*"I have found **Bob's attention to detail** and his ability to fine tune his seminars to match the time frame and needs of the audience to be a valuable asset to our educational program."* **Patsy Schell**, *Executive Director Surrey Chamber of Commerce*

*"Great seeing you in Cancun and congratulations on a job well done. **The seminar was a great success! Your humorous and conversational style was a tremendous asset.** It is my sincere hope that we can be associated again at future seminars."* **Donald MacPherson**, *Attorney At Law, Phoenix, Arizona*

"What a great conference. *It was a great pleasure meeting with you at the Ritz Carlton, Cancun and I shall look forward to hopefully welcoming you and your family in Dublin, Ireland someday."* **A. Paul Ryan**, *Petronva Corporation, Dublin, Ireland*

*"Congratulations on the **Spirit of CAPS Award**. You have worked long and hard on behalf of CAPS …**helped many speakers including me** and richly deserve this award. Well done my friend."* **Peter Legge**, *CSP, Hof, CPAE*

*"I had the pleasure of hearing and watching Bob Hooey deliver a keynote speech several years ago when he gave a presentation at a Toastmasters International Convention. **Bob impressed me greatly with his professionalism, energy, and ability to connect with his audience while giving them value.** I heartily recommend this talented speaker and 'Idea Man' to all who want to move to the next level."* **Dr. Dilip Abayasekara, DTM, Accredited Speaker,** *Past President, Toastmasters International*

*"I attended **Speaking for Success** in Edmonton. **The mark of a true leader is someone who will lay down their own pride to teach all they know to their potential successors.** To be taught by a man of his caliber was an honor whether you're a beginner like myself or a professional; the experience is well worth it! To Bob - it truly was an honor to meet you. Stay humble and enjoy the great success."* ***Samantha McLeod***

Bob's B.E.S.T. publications

Bob is a *prolific* author who has been capturing and sharing his wisdom and experience in print and electronic formats for the past fifteen plus years. In addition to the following publications, several of them best sellers, he has written for consumer, corporate, professional associations, trade, and on-line publications. He has been engaged to write and assist on publications by other best-selling writers and successful companies.

His publications are listed to give you an idea of the scope and topics he writes about. Bob's **B**usiness **E**nhancement **S**uccess **T**ools.

Leadership, business, and career development series

- **Running TOO Fast** (8th edition 2022)
- **Legacy of Leadership** (6th edition 2023)
- **Make ME Feel Special!** (6th edition 2022)
- **Why Didn't I 'THINK' of That?** (6th edition 2022)
- **Speaking for Success!** (10th edition 2023)
- **THINK Beyond the First Sale** (3rd edition 2022)
- **Prepare Yourself to Win!** (3rd edition 2017)
- **The early years… 1998-2009 - A Tip of the Hat collection** (2023)
- **The saga continues… 2010-2019 – A Tip of the Hat collection** (2023)

Bob's Mini-book success series

- **The Courage to Lead!** (4th edition 2024)
- **Creative Conflict** (3rd edition 2024)
- **Get to YES!** (5th edition 2023)
- **THINK Before You Ink!** (3rd edition 2024)
- **Running to Win!** (2nd edition 2024)
- **Generate More Sales** (5th edition 2023)
- **Unleash your Business Potential** (3rd edition 2024)
- **Maximize Meetings** (new for 2024)
- **Learn to Listen** (2nd edition 2017)

- **Creativity Counts!** (updated 2024)
- **Create Your Future!** (3rd edition 2024)

Kindle Shorts (2018-2023) new epub series

- **SPEAK!**
- **LEAD!**
- **SERVE!**
- **CREATE!**
- **CONFLICT!**
- **TIME!**
- **More to come in 2024**

Bob's Pocket Wisdom series

- **Pocket Wisdom for Speakers** (updated 2019)
- **Pocket Wisdom for Leaders – Power of One!** (updated 2019)
- Additional PW books are coming as ebooks in 2020

Co-authored books created by Bob

- Quantum Success – 3 volume series (2006 – to be updated in 2024)
- **In The Company of Leaders (95th anniversary Edition 2019)**
- Foundational Success (2nd Edition 2013)

Visit: www.SuccessPublications.ca for more information on Bob's publications and other success resources.

A final note as 2019 winds to a close. Creating this two-book project for 2020 release has been an amazing opportunity to go back over 22 years of living, family, friends, and, of course adventures. It is fun to realize I learned to write and was able to share a few ideas with you as well as audiences around the world. My thanks to all of you.

A Tip of the Hat to everyone who made me smile, think, stretch, and grow over the past two decades. You have enriched my life and I am forever indebted to you. I take you with me in my heart as I continue my adventures around the globe.

Thanks for reading
The early years... 1998-2009

Each time I prepare to step on the stage; each time I sit down to write or in this case to re-write, I am challenged to deliver something that will be of use-it-now value to my audience/reader.

- I ask myself, *"If I was reading this, what value would I be looking for?"*
- As well as, *"Why is this relevant to me, today?"*

These two questions help to keep me focused and clear on my objectives. They help to remind me to dig into my experiences, stories, examples, and research to provide solid information that will be of benefit and help our readers, when they apply it, succeed. That can be an exciting challenge!

I trust we have done that for you in this updated primer on enhanced business success. *'A Tip of the Hat collection'* is my attempt to capture some of the lessons learned first-hand from observing and working with some tremendously effective leaders, retailers, service providers, and business owners.

Bob 'Idea Man' Hooey, 2011 Spirit of CAPS recipient
www.ideaman.net
www.BobHooey.training
www.HaveMouthWillTravel.com

Connect with me on:
- **Facebook:** www.facebook.com/bob.hooey
- **LinkedIn:** www.linkedin.com/in/canadianideamanbobhooey
- **YouTube:** www.youtube.com/ideamanbob
- **Smashwords:** www.smashwords.com/profile/view/Hooey
- **Follow me on Twitter:** @IdeamanHooey
- **Snail mail:** Box 10, Egremont, Alberta, T0A0Z0, CANADA
- **Amazon:** www.amazon.com/Bob-Idea-Man-Hooey/e/B00FACOHNY

Engage Bob for your leaders and their teams

"I have been so excited working with Bob Hooey, as he has given inspiration and motivation to our leadership team members. Both at the Brick Warehouse – Alberta and at Art Van Furniture – Michigan; with his years of experience in working with business executives and his humorous and delightful packaging of his material, he makes learning with Bob a real joy. But most importantly, anyone who comes in contact with his material is the better for it."
Kim Yost, *retired* CEO Art Van Furniture, *former* CEO The Brick

Motivate your teams, your employees, and your leaders to 'productively' grow and 'profitably' succeed!

- Protect your conference investment - leverage your training dollars.
- Enhance your professional career and sell more products and services.
- Equip and motivate your leaders and their teams to grow and succeed, 'even' in tough times!
- Leverage your time to enhance your skills, equip your teams, and better serve your clients.
- Leverage your leadership and investment of time to leave a significant legacy within your organization and life!

Call today to engage best-selling author, award winning, inspirational leadership keynote speaker, leaders success coach, and employee development trainer, **Bob 'Idea Man' Hooey** and his innovative, audience based, results-focused, **Ideas At Work!** for your next company, convention, leadership, staff, training, or association event. You'll be glad you did!

Call 1-780-736-0009 to connect with Bob 'Idea Man' Hooey today!

Learn more about Bob at: www.ideaman.net

 Visit: www.SuccessPublications.ca/BusinessSuccess-Tips.html for special business building success tips, just for you.

www.ingramcontent.com/pod-product-compliance
Lightning Source LLC
Chambersburg PA
CBHW071010120626
46546CB00003B/1027